The T

A volume in the British Monarchy series, which
also includes:

CHRISTOPHER MORRIS

The Tudors

FONTANA/COLLINS

First published by B. T. Batsford Ltd. 1955
First issued in The Fontana Library 1966
Eighth Impression May 1972

© Christopher Morris December 1955

Printed in Great Britain
Collins Clear-Type Press
London and Glasgow

L. & M.

FOR ANN AND CHARLES

CONTENTS

ILLUSTRATIONS

PREFACE

This book is neither a text-book of Tudor history nor a series of narrative biographies. What I have attempted is an essay on the personalities of the Tudor monarchs and on their impact upon English history. I see no need to apologise for thinking that, even in these days, history may still be about individual people. Much Tudor history, especially in its economic, constitutional, diplomatic and theological aspects, has been inevitably and quite deliberately omitted —except where it is touched on in my two introductory chapters.

The book is the fruit of reflections prompted by a good many years of teaching Tudor history, which is of course the best way of learning it. I do not know how far what I have written can be dignified or denigrated with the title of "original research", since I doubt whether it is any longer possible, in writing history, to be original and at the same time truthful; and I doubt whether I have mentioned a single fact that is not already known to some historian. But at least I have used the contemporary sources that lie, or ought to lie, behind the text-books.

I have not attempted to give references for statements of what is well-known or easily verified. I have, however, intentionally given full references concerning Edward VI, because there is no readily available standard life of him. I have also fully documented my chapter on Elizabeth, because the standard biographies of her give no references at all.

For obvious reasons, my chapter on Edward VI has had to deal reasonably fully with his two "protectors", Somerset and Dudley; but I have not thought it necessary to deal in the same way with Wolsey and Cromwell, with Gardiner and Pole, or with Walsingham and Burghley.

7

Because he was known successively as " Lisle ", " Warwick ", and " Northumberland ", I have referred to John Dudley as " Dudley ". His son Robert, though he was not an earl till 1564, I have for obvious convenience called " Leicester ". William Cecil did not become Lord Burghley till 1571 and therefore I have generally called him " Cecil ". His son I have called " Robert Cecil " as he was not made Earl of Salisbury until 1605.

I have treated Elizabeth at greater length than her predecessors because her reign was longer and perhaps even more important, and also because we have a considerably greater bulk of evidence about her personality.

I have adopted modern spelling for all quotations, as I wished the Tudors to appear real people and not merely " quaint ".

It is a pleasure to record my debts. I have learnt much about Tudor economics from Mr John Saltmarsh, much about Tudor art from Mr Kenneth Harrison, and much about Tudor government from Dr Geoffrey Elton. I am also indebted to Dr Elton's infallible judgment as to what sources are unreliable; and I greatly regret that I have not been able to read his forthcoming history of Tudor England before rashly committing my own views to print.

What I owe to my wife, a considerable scholar in Tudor literature, is beyond computation. I should have been equally lost without her stylistic and without her common sense; and without her encouragement the book would never have been written.

I am also deeply grateful to my College for not overwhelming me with pupils during the years in which I have been working on this book; and, in particular, for the courtesy of the College Council in allowing me to use a picture that has never been reproduced before.

CHRISTOPHER MORRIS

Summer, 1955

ACKNOWLEDGMENTS

The pictures of Edward VI, from the portrait after Hans Holbein, and The Princess Elizabeth, aged about 13, are reproduced by Gracious Permission of Her Majesty the Queen.

The Author and Publishers would like to thank the following for permission to reproduce the illustrations appearing in this book:

The Earl of Bradford and the Walker Art Gallery, Liverpool, for the portrait of Anne Boleyn; Lord Metheun, for the portrait of Elizabeth I with Time and Death; H. Clifford Smith Esq., for the portrait of Henry VIII aged 25.

The Ashmolean Museum, Oxford, for the drawing of "The Gorgeous Palaces": Hampton Court; Bibliotèque Méjanes, Aix, for the drawing of Henry VIII as a child; the Trustees of the British Museum, for the drawing of "The Cloud-Capp'd Towers": Nonesuch Palace; and the portrait of Henry VIII in old age; R. P. Howgrave-Graham, Muniment Room and Library, Westminster Abbey, for the sculpture of Henry VII from the funeral effigy in Westminster Abbey; King's College, Cambridge, for the stained glass painting of King Solomon; the National Portrait Gallery, for the portraits of Henry VII holding a Tudor Rose and Catherine of Aragon; Jean Roubier, for the medals of Henry VIII and Mary I; the Society of Antiquaries of London, for the portrait of Mary I by Hans Eworth; the Trustees of the Victoria and Albert Museum, for the terracotta bust of Henry VII by Pietro Torrigiano and the miniature of Elizabeth I by Nicholas Hilliard.

CHAPTER I

CULTURE, POLITICS AND
THE TUDORS

If an educated man was asked what were the most important things produced by Tudor England he might well say
they were the plays of Shakespeare. It is not so certain that
this was Shakespeare's view. He did not trouble himself
overmuch about their publication; and he may have valued
them largely for the power they gave him to buy a coat-of-
arms and the biggest house in Stratford. There is something
in Pope's view that Shakespeare

> For gain, not glory, winged his roving flight
> And grew immortal in his own despite.

To the modern mind it is constantly surprising to find how
unselfconscious about their " culture " men have been, even
at those moments in history when cultural achievement
has been highest. Indeed a culture that has become intro-
spective and too much aware that it is " culture " may be
well on the road to decline. Perhaps no true artist is an
" aesthete " and perhaps the arts flourish best when they
are least self-conscious and most utilitarian. " Men cease to
build beautiful churches when they have lost happiness in
building shops."[1]

Most mediaeval art was anonymous; and Aeschylus,
when he composed his own epitaph, wished nothing to be
recorded of him except that he had fought at Marathon.
Pericles, in his funeral oration, says little to the Athenians
of their culture. The elegance of their domestic architecture,
he says, merely suffices to drive away the spleen and to
provide some relaxation after the real business of life. And
if he praises their pursuit of truth and beauty, he does so
because it has not led them into effeminacy or decadence.
He does not mention poetry except to say that Athens needs

no Homer nor any other poet to immortalise her, since poets can only charm for the moment and can only create illusions which melt at the touch of hard fact. It is in the hard facts of her wealth and power, of her military and political achievement, that Athens must take her proper pride. There is no suggestion that a poet's words can out-live marble or the gilded monuments of princes, still less that Athens may be remembered for her culture long after her empire has fallen into dust.

Tudor Englishmen agreed with Pericles and not with us. When Shakespeare predicted the immortality of his "powerful rime", he may have been very far from sincere. It was, after all, a literary conceit borrowed from Horace, and the proper thing to say in a sonnet to one's mistress's, or one's patron's, eyebrow. It is just as likely that Shakespeare thought of himself as

> a poor player
> That struts and frets his hour upon the stage,
> And then is heard no more,

and that he believed "the best in this kind are but shadows".

Dramatists in Shakespeare's day cannot have hoped for more than contemporary fame. The initial run of a play averaged some five performances, relatively few plays were revived, and very few were printed. Ben Jonson was thought eccentric and arrogant for publishing plays under the title of his *Works*. No playwright in his senses could have supposed himself to be writing "for all time". No wonder that poets and dramatists included in their works political sermons on issues that were certain to become quickly out of date. The Elizabethans lived in the present, and lived for politics, perhaps more than any men since the ancient Greeks have ever done. It would have been useless to tell them that art is long and that life, especially political life, is short.

In any case, Pericles may have been right. The greatest poets have not lived in ivory towers. Dante and Milton

cared passionately about politics; and Shelley once wrote :
" I consider poetry very subordinate to moral and political
science, and if I were well, certainly I would aspire to the
latter."[2] Often enough the kind of scepticism which regards
all political action as ultimately futile will enervate and
sterilise all other activities of the human spirit.

Nor, unfortunately, have all the political poets been
idealists striving to lift some load from the shoulders of the
oppressed. There is also the poetry of the strong man rejoic-
ing in his strength, and poets may easily conceive of themselves as an *élite* of superior beings entitled to spurn the
masses. Hazlitt thought that " the language of poetry
naturally falls in with the language of power. . . . Poetry is
right-royal. It puts the individual for the species, the one
above the infinite many, might before right. A lion hunting
a flock of sheep or a herd of wild asses is a more poetical
subject than they; and we ever take part with the lordly
beast, because our vanity or some other feeling makes us
disposed to place ourselves in the situation of the strongest
party. . . . The love of power in ourselves and the admiration
of it in others are both natural to man : the one makes him
a tyrant, the other a slave. Wrong dressed out in pride,
pomp and circumstance, has more attraction than absolute
right." Certainly the Elizabethan dramatists would seem to
bear Hazlitt out. They produced a long line of hero-villains
from Marlowe's Jew of Malta to Jonson's Volpone; and it
is clear that both dramatists and audience liked to watch
the cat among the pigeons.

Some of the poets—among them Ralegh, Spenser,
Sidney—openly sought place and power for themselves.
They believed that poetry could and should be politically
useful—useful not only in the training of a governing class,
but useful also as a means for rising in the world. In the
opening scene of *Timon of Athens* it is the poet who paints
the great image of men seeking to climb Fortune's Hill.
The arts were social accomplishments in an age when
accomplishment could open many doors. It was a proof of

" worth ", of " virtue " in the Tudor sense of virtuosity; it stood warrant for a man's claim to preferment. It was a way of catching a patron's favour and attested the all-round ability that might do a patron good service. Henry VIII chose impoverished scholars for much of his administrative, diplomatic and propaganda work. Sir Christopher Hatton first caught Queen Elizabeth's eye through his proficiency in dancing. The conventions of high society were stilted and artificial to an extraordinary degree and the ability to pun, to turn a euphuistic compliment or to improvise a sonnet carried immense weight. And since the command of an army or a fleet might depend on court favour, it was necessary for ambitious soldiers and sailors to hang about the court and learn to do as courtiers did.

Besides, it was an age of great social and economic fluidity. Fortunes could be made and lost with remarkable speed. If a man was rich and accomplished, it suggested that he was well brought up and that his fortune was neither too newly made nor yet unmerited. If a man was poor and accomplished, it suggested that his poverty was undeserved, that his abilities warranted a better turn of Fortune's wheel. Certainly lack of accomplishment argued a disgraceful origin. In the preface to *A Plaine and Easie Instruction to Practicall Musicke* (1597) by the composer Morley, a man tells how he was accused of " discourtesy " because he could not join in a musical discussion after a banquet, and how, when he could not sing a part at sight from a " music book ", " everyone began to wonder. Yea, some whispered to others, demanding how I was brought up."

But music in Tudor England was more than a court accomplishment. It cannot have been any snobbish desire to climb or impress which made Drake and Sir Humphrey Gilbert and John Davis find room for a small orchestra in their tiny ships on transatlantic voyages. Nor was it a desire to prove himself well-bred that made Bottom call for the tongs and the bones. Nor again was it ostentation which caused Elizabethan barber-surgeons to provide citherns for the use of waiting clients, who are nowadays supplied with illustrated papers. The truth is that in the Tudor period the English people were more musical than they have ever been. They also produced more and better music than any European people had yet done. The facts are indisputable and also unaccountable; they are facts that the historian had better not try to explain, since there is no known law governing the appearance of musical inspiration.

There is one inference which the historian must be particularly careful not to draw. Music may be soft and sweet, and on occasion soothing to the savage breast. Yet many song-birds are exceedingly fierce, and there was little softness about Tudor Englishmen. Adam Smith did not find it surprising that "the musical education of the Greeks had no great effect in mending their morals", since "music and dancing are the great amusements of almost all barbarious nations".[3] The historian Polybius records that the Arcadians, more than any other Greeks, made music an integral part of their education, and that among them "no one can disclaim the knowledge of how to sing because all are forced to learn". Their object, he says, "was not the gratification of luxury and extravagance. They saw that Arcadia was a nation of workers, that the life of the people was laborious and hard, and that in consequence of the coldness and gloom which were the prevailing features of a great part of the country, the general character of the people was austere. And it was with a view to softening and tempering this natural ruggedness and rusticity that they . . . did everything they could to humanise their souls by the civilising and softening influence of such culture."[4]

Without being so fully deliberate in cultivating softening influences, Tudor England had something in common with Arcadia; and certainly Tudor Englishmen could be as bleak and stark as any Arcadian. There were indeed many Philistines among them—even among the educated—who alleged, as Sir Philip Sidney tells us, that "before poets began to be in price, our nation hath set their heart's delight upon action and not upon imagination, rather doing things worthy to be written than writing things fit to be done." But Sidney could reply " certain it is that, in our plainest homeliness, yet never was the Albion nation without poetry "; and he could assert from his own military experience that " poetry is the companion of the camp. I dare undertake *Orlando Furioso* or honest *King Arthur* will never displease a soldier."[5]

The Renaissance humanist Sir Thomas Elyot, in his *Boke of the Governour* (1531), advocated knowledge of all the liberal arts for the young nobleman, although he showed some signs of fear that his pupils might grow too soft. He regretted that some authorities in his day " without shame dare affirm that to a great gentleman it is a notable reproach to be well learned and to be called a great clerk."[6] Yet he himself could say " it were . . . better that no music were taught to a noble man, than, by exact knowledge thereof, he should have therein inordinate delight and by that be illected to wantonness, abandoning gravity and the necessary care and office in the public weal to him committed."[7] Admittedly Elyot thought football too rough for noblemen, "wherein is nothing but beastly fury and extreme violence, whereof proceedeth hurt; and consequently rancour and malice do remain with them that be wounded; wherefore it is to be put in perpetual silence."[8] On the other hand, most forms of hunting were too soft. "The hunting of red deer and fallow might be a great part of semblable exercise used by noble men . . . if they would use but a few number of hounds only to . . . rouse the game and . . . give knowledge which way it fleeth; the remnant of the disport to be in pursuing with javelins and other weapons in manner of war." Fox-hunting was " not to be compared with the other hunting in commodity of exercise," while " hunting of the hare with greyhounds is a right good solace for men that be studious, of them to whom nature hath not given personage or courage apt for the

wars. And also for gentlewomen which fear neither sun nor
wind for appairing of their beauty. And peradventure they
should be thus at less idle than they should be in their
chambers."[9]

Sir Thomas Elyot need not have feared, for neither music
nor poetry, nor even beagling, were to make men soft. The
men of Tudor England could outface the block and the
stake or the horrors and hazards of a long sea voyage. In
war they were world-famous for their bravery, not to say
foolhardiness. They sought the bubble reputation quite
literally in the cannon's mouth. An army chaplain relates
that at the siege of Ostend (1601-2) " an English gentleman
of about twenty-three years of age, in a sally forth, had
one of his arms shot off by a cannon; which, taking up he
brought back with him into the town unto the chirurgeon;
and coming to his lodging shewed it, saying, ' Behold the
arm which but at dinner helped its fellow.' This he did
and endured, without the least fainting or so much as
reposing upon his bed."[10] The English could be brash as
well as brave. Perhaps Ralegh was so when he held his
fire, as his ship was sailing into Cadiz, and answered the
Spanish salvo " with the blare of a trumpet . . . disdaining
to shoot one piece at any one or all of those esteemed
dreadful monsters ".

Perhaps Tudor toughness was a necessary condition without which there could have been no Tudor culture. It is
sometimes necessary to be strong in order to bring forth
sweetness; and creative power in the arts is not always given
to men by way of compensation for not being able to do
anything else. Very often it is born of self-confidence in
a man or in a whole community. It can be the surplus
overflow of temperaments highly charged with an energy
convertible into many forms. Men and communities that
have grown vigorous are more likely than not to be
vigorous in more than one direction. In a balanced and
integrated society the boundaries between life and letters,
or between thought and action, are apt to become blurred.

Everyone, including the plain blunt man, may find it easier to be articulate. Tudor poets went to the wars and made their mark in them; and Tudor soldiers and sailors had a habit of writing pregnant and evocative prose. In a hasty despatch to Walsingham in the middle of the fight with the Armada, Drake could write : " We have the army of Spain before us and mind with the Grace of God to wrestle a fall with him . . . God grant you have a good eye to the Duke of Parma : for with the Grace of God, if we live, I doubt not but, ere it be long, so to handle the matter with the Duke of Sidonia as he shall wish himself at St Mary Port among his orange trees." Modern military despatches have, as a rule, neither that confidence nor yet those cadences. Never have the relations between Martha and Mary been closer than they were in Tudor England : Mary did some house-work and Martha found time for dreams and contemplation.

Yet the dreams and contemplation were seldom intro-spective. Indeed it has been argued that Tudor men and women talked and wrote as though they had virtually no " inner life ". Like a colonial people, obsessed with the material problems of carving out a new life on a moving " frontier ", they had no time for emotional refinements. It would often be impossible to say from its content that a Tudor lyric was written by one poet rather than another. The love which the poets apostrophised might almost be called a communal emotion. It was considered as a passion felt by all men in much the same way : and, until Sidney wrote *Astrophel and Stella*, it was rare for a poet to analyse what made his passion different from another's. The anatomising of private emotion came in only with Donne and the Jacobeans. Indeed the Elizabethan seems hardly ever to have wanted to be alone. Hamlet aroused the king's suspicions by his solitude; and in more than one Elizabethan play the villain is made to show his villainy by claiming to be self-sufficient and appearing as the unsociable or unsocial man.[11]

There were Tudor writers on psychology but they wrote
in terms of the "humours" and "elements" that all men
had in common. "Choler" and "melancholy" were
studied for their common properties and symptoms, just as
a doctor first studies what are the universal symptoms of a
physical disease. There was little belief even in the individual will; and men were deemed to be more or less helpless
once they were possessed by a ruling passion. An Elizabethan audience would hardly expect Othello to master his
jealousy, Macbeth his ambition or Antony his lust.[12] Much,
it is true was written of "the Soul"; but it meant the Soul
which makes all men alike and all men different from beasts
rather than the Soul which makes one man a different
person from another. The popularity of books on stock
"characters" and "characteristics", by such men as
Joseph Hall or Nicholas Breton, is certainly significant. We
are mistaken if we exaggerate the individuality of the
characters in Elizabethan drama—even in Shakespearean
drama. It may be that the sixteenth-century lack of interest
in men's private feelings had something to do with the
cruelty and heartlessness of the age, and that the same lack
of introspection helped to make possible the stoicism displayed by so many of the victims of that cruelty.

Few men of the sixteenth century can be called "soulful".
Even their religion, by contrast both with the century
before and the century after, was singularly unmystical.
There was something robust and hearty, something
extroverted, even in the Tudor Protestant's sense of sin.
He had more a sense of mankind's sin than of his own. And
no Tudor religious writer has left any record of "the dark
night of the soul".

Nor were the frontiers between soul and body, between
mind and matter, very clearly mapped. A man's temperament was jovial, mercurial, or saturnine in accordance with
the physical location of the planets at his birth : and if a
noble mind like Lear's was overthrown, the audience would
almost expect an accompanying convulsion of the physical

elements. Mind too had little pre-eminence over body, or intellectual achievement over physical. Sidney and Ralegh impressed their contemporaries as much by their athletic or martial prowess as by their intellects. Hamlet may well have done so too. " It is not a mind, not a body, that we have to educate, but a man and we cannot divide him." So wrote Richard Mulcaster, Spenser's headmaster at the Merchant Taylors'. All the accomplishments were to be sought after, and all the arts, not least the art of war. Roger Ascham, that other great Tudor educationalist, was of much the same mind. He regretted that " the young gentlemen of England go so unwillingly to school and run so fast to the stable "; but he also said : " I do not mean that young gentlemen should always be poring over a book." They " should use and delight in all courtly exercises and gentle-manlike pastimes . . . for the Muses, besides learning, were also ladies of dancing, mirth and minstrelsy : Apollo was god of shooting and author of cunning playing upon instruments. Pallas also was lady mistress in wars."[18] There is a real though very subtle connection between the arts and political and military morale. At the height of the Dutchmen's maritime supremacy, their Admiralty employed the two Van der Veldes as official war artists and provided them with a small ship from which to paint the naval victories of Holland.

By the time that Drake wrote his Armada despatch English society had become vigorous and confident, balanced and integrated, in a very peculiar degree. From small beginnings, Tudor England had developed considerable economic and military power. Even more markedly, her society had changed from one that was top-heavy, rickety and unstable to one that was broadly based, with closed ranks and high morale, at once solid and elastic, at once firmly rooted and adventurous, realistic and yet with a sense of exaltation, serious and yet often gay. Much was due to natural resources, both economic and psychological, released for the first time. Much more than is generally recognised was due to the reigning dynasty itself. It was a period in which politics really mattered and government could do some real good. The new wealth could not be accumulated without the building up of credit and security; and side by side with the newly rich there was a "new poor" who created serious social problems. The new energies needed much conservation, much canalising, and much restraint. The new national power could so easily have been squandered or brought to bear at the wrong time upon the wrong objectives. The new enthusiasms could have turned sour and fanatical and bred cancers in the commonwealth. There was an "old religion" which had to be reconciled with the new. The new society required leadership if it was not to become quite irresponsible. There was native genius in the English people, but genius needs looking after. It is not always good at managing its own affairs, and it requires particularly good housekeeping if it is to avoid either malnutrition or over-riotous living. Someone must see that it gets regular meals and put it to bed when it gets drunk; someone must pay its bills and find a market for its products. Someone must keep it tidy and see that it does not waste itself, just as Madame Cézanne had to collect her husband's discarded canvases from the fields and hedges.

Tudor taste was still very Gothic; it was a taste for the excrescent, the florid, the flamboyant. It ran to profusion. It could not resist filling all available spaces with arabesque and ornament; it had to be lavish and garish in display. The dramatists ignored the unities and mouthed much needless rhetoric. *The Faerie Queene* and Sidney's *Arcadia* are endless rivers that wind in labyrinthine deviations and constantly overflow their banks. Tudor costumes were fantastic, grandiose and ornate. The masques and "insubstantial pageants" were weighed down with elaborate, over-ingenious allegory. The "gorgeous palaces" sprawled over their grounds and were plastered with timbering, pargeting and all kinds of fancy work. Somewhere in this ramshackle, dishevelled, raffish world some principle of order and coherence was required. Somewhere behind the stucco there had to be firm structural support. Within the slashed sleeves and the trunk hose there had to be real bone and sinew. All such coherence, structure, sinew had to be provided by the frame of government.

In innumerable ways the sovereign could harness the new energies, call a halt to extravagance or control the centri-fugal loyalties of the time. The gentry had to pay some taxes and perform some social duties. If too much silk and satin were imported, it might damage English broadcloth. If too much meat was eaten, the fisheries might suffer. If too much labour went into mansion-building, the roads and bridges might not be repaired. If too much land was enclosed for sheep-walk or for deer-park there might not be enough for tillage. The West Country privateers could not be allowed to embroil the country prematurely with the King of Spain. Religious enthusiasts could not be allowed to cause breaches of the peace or of political unity. The House of Commons could not be allowed to discuss affairs it did not understand and for which it was not responsible. Potentially turbulent nobles had to be induced to come to court, where Henry VII could watch them narrowly and fleece them of their surplus riches; where Henry VIII could overawe them or appease them with monastery land; where Elizabeth could keep them dangling in hopes of preferment, of monopolies, of an Irish plantation, or even of her hand.

The Tudor century was a century of revolution, and each one of the great changes that were going on meant more work for the government. The price-rise, rack-renting, enclosures, the dissolution of the monasteries, the cutting-down of liveried retainers, all contributed to unemploy-ment; and this threw upon government shoulders the task of sifting the genuine hard case from work-shy rogues and vagabonds. New developments in mining and in industry, following the decay and abolition of the guilds, caused the government to concern itself with standards of workmanship and conditions of employment. Overseas expansion and new vents for trade forced the government to ponder over the amount of bullion exported or the amount of corn imported. The growth of London and recurrent dire visitations of the plague led the government to insist on the keeping of the first vital statistics—the mortality bills. The government had to maintain some remote control over the distribution of monastery land, and had later to see that the Crown got its fair share of captured Spanish treasure. New developments in naval warfare required provision for the latest types of ships and guns. Threats of invasion necessitated keeping the militia in something like fighting trim, albeit with bows and arrows. The same threats, together with factious plots at home, produced a more and more elaborate system of intelligence and espionage. The increasing complication of international affairs brought much more activity for diplomatic agents; and contacts had to be made even with the Grand Turk or with the Tsar. Revolutions in Scotland and the first serious chance to detach the Scots from France demanded much of the government's attention; while only ceaseless vigilance could prevent Ireland from becoming a running sore that drained away irreplaceable life and money. The new religious alignments called for strict government control of the pulpit and the press, and, sometimes, for an eye to be kept upon the universities. Above all, no Tudor government was ever free from worry about the succession to the throne.

The situation demanded, and indeed obtained, a " welfare state " at least in rudimentary form.* That anything of the kind should have been evolved is a staggering achievement in view of the resources and machinery at the government's disposal—perhaps even more astounding in view of the prejudices which had to be overcome.

The essence of the problem was that almost all govern-

* Even a modern government might hesitate to do as the Tudors did when they compelled all their subjects to wear hats in order to safeguard the manufacture of felt.

ment had to be government by amateurs. The Tudors did not possess and could not afford to possess the common tools of the true despot. There was no standing army and, even though the Crown had a monopoly of the manufacture of artillery, Tudor roads hardly allowed the movement of guns large enough to knock down a castle. There was no police force. There were only Dogberry and Verges, the petty constable and his watch.

And Dogberry and Verges could be met with in real life, as we know from Dr A. L. Rowse's discovery of a letter sent by Burghley to Walsingham in 1586 when the hunt was up for the conspirators in the Babington plot.

" Sir ", he writes, " As I came from London homeward in my coach I saw at every town's end the number of ten or twelve standing with long staves, and until I came to Enfield I thought no other of them but that they had stayed for avoiding of the rain, or to drink at some alehouse, for so they did stand under pentices [penthouses] at alehouses. But at Enfield finding a dozen in a plump, when there was no rain, I bethought myself that they were appointed as watchmen, for the apprehending of such as are missing. And thereupon I called some of them to me apart and asked them wherefore they stood there. And one of them answered ' To take three young men '. And demanding how they should know the persons, one answered with these words, ' Marry, my lord, by intelligence of their favour.' ' What mean you by that?' quoth I. ' Marry,' said they, ' one of the parties hath a hooked nose.' ' And have you,' quoth I, ' no other mark?' ' No,' saith they. And then I asked who appointed them. And they answered one Banks, a head constable, whom I willed to be sent to me. Surely, sir, whoever had the charge from you hath used the matter negligently. For these watchmen stand so openly in plumps as no suspected person will come near them; and if they be no better instructed but to find three persons by one of them having a hooked nose, they may miss thereof. And thus I think good to advertise you, that the Justices that had the charge, as I think, may use the matter more circumspectly."[14]

Above all, there was only the barest skeleton of a professional civil service. There was a handful of more or less permanent clerks, expert in legal or financial business; and there were certain remarkable diplomats and trained administrators, like Sir William Petre and Sir John Mason (the son of a cowherd), who made themselves so indispensable that they survived every change of government and served on the Councils of every sovereign from the last years of Henry VIII to the first years of Elizabeth : and there was Sir Ralph Sadler who was a Councillor to all save Mary. But nearly all of such men were virtually unsalaried and had to be paid in perquisites and pickings.

The old feudal ruling class, who remained surprisingly popular in many quarters, were on the whole opposed to Tudor policy. They had bled themselves white and lost caste during the Wars of the Roses and, in any case, they had for long signally failed to do much ruling. The " new men ", the squires and business men and lawyers, were anxious enough to be allowed to rule but needed much restraint and much training for responsibility. Many among them had eyes only for the spoils of office. For some time considerable reliance had to be placed on churchmen, as in the Middle Ages, for doing governmental work. They had the education and often the administrative experience required. But the Reformation lowered clerical prestige, rendered the conservative half of the clergy disloyal, and also led to much insistence on churchmen's attending to their own proper business. Wolsey and Gardiner were the last of a long line of mediaeval clerical prime ministers. Cranmer did not attain the same pre-eminence, still less Archbishop Parker, and Elizabeth had no bishop on her Council until Archbishop Whitgift was put there in 1586.

One of the most delicate tasks that faced the Tudors, therefore, was the creation and education of a new ruling class and the retention of its loyalty. The new men had to be prevented from moving up too fast or too far. The drive and efficiency in economic matters which brought them their wealth and power also made them harsh to their tenants and contemptuous of the common people. There was much crying out among the frogs for the return of King Log and the displacement of King Stork. The poor had some reason to complain. They made too much, perhaps, of the dissolution of the monasteries, for the social service of the monks has been exaggerated. But did the new possessors of monastery land do any more? There is some reason to doubt it; and now and then one of the new men would give the game away. " Do ye not know that the King's Grace hath put down all the houses of monks, friars and nuns? Therefore now is the time come that we gentlemen will pull down the houses of such poor knaves as ye be." The words are those of John Palmer, Sheriff of Surrey and Sussex, in answer to a petition for the return of peasants' holdings converted to his own use.[15]

The peasants were sometimes ill-informed as to the causes of their troubles but their very ignorance made them the more dangerous; and more than once they came very near to calling the whole Tudor bluff. The Cornish peasantry rose, not for the last time, in 1497 and were only defeated in the London suburbs. The Norfolk peasants rose against Edward VI's evil counsellors. The Kentish peasants rose against Queen Mary, occupied Southwark and Knightsbridge, and were only turned back at Charing Cross. On two great occasions, in the Pilgrimage of Grace and again in 1569, the North Country peasants rose—to see their leaders throw away their chances when everything was touch and go. The boasted freedom of Tudor England from armed rebellion and from civil war was merely relative freedom, as compared with earlier centuries and as compared with other countries. England was spared only from *successful* rebellion and only by the narrowest of margins.

There were other reasons, hardly less cogent, for not

giving the new men too much power or freedom. If they had no more worlds to conquer they might cease to look to the Crown for further advancement; and self-sufficiency might make them into rebels themselves. History was to prove this when the grandsons of Burghley and of Walsingham fought against Charles I. Although it was eventually the new men who made England great, their interests did not invariably coincide with the national interest. They could not be allowed to make England so radically Protestant as to foment civil war or to court foreign invasion. On the other hand, when it did become necessary to prepare for war with Spain, the City merchants did much to delay open hostilities and to sabotage the war effort, in order to retain their trade with Spanish Flanders. The "City" has not invariably put patriotism before its own interests and has sometimes shown a propensity for trading with the king's enemies. Did it not, under Charles II, embroil England in an indefensible war against her natural allies, the Dutch? A wise government will know that economic threats to our "big business" and military threats to our actual existence are not always identical and do not always come from the same quarter.

The new ruling class needed considerable political education; and the place where many of them had their schooling was the House of Commons. The House had many uses, not the least of which was its service as a kind of ministry of information. The information flowed in two directions: from the Commons the government could learn about local requirements, local grievances and local resources, while at the same time the Commons could learn from the Privy Councillors who sat among them what the government's policy was, and what support, moral and material, was expected of them. The House of Commons was virtually a house of J.P.'s; and in the House the justices could be told the whys and wherefors of the laws they were required to execute; and they could be told, as they were by Elizabeth herself in 1593, that as justices they were expected to make them " living laws ". Without such co-operation, laws could easily become dead or could easily be administered in a spirit contrary to the government's intention.

A case in point is the legislation against recusancy. Obviously the dangerous recusants were the rich and great ones; but few magistrates were willing to enforce the law very stringently against their social equals. As a result it was mostly the poor and harmless recusant who was penalised. " By this statute there is constraint to come to divine service; and for neglect all must pay. . . . The poor commonalty, whose strength and quietness is the strength and quietness of us all, he only shall be punished, he vexed. For will any think that the justice of peace will contest with so good a man as himself?" So spoke Dr Bond, Member for Taunton, in 1601; and it is significant that this speaker was howled down by a House that would tolerate no criticism of the J.P.s.[16]

The same debate in the Commons produced a complaint that some justices were not above altering a neighbour's assessment for subsidy taxes in return for a consideration. Another speaker also drew attention to the well-known practice by which magistrates and officers could draw " dead-pays " for militiamen who existed only in the muster roll. Like Falstaff, they " misused the king's press damn-ably ", enlisting those most likely or best able to buy them-selves out of military service.[17] There is indeed plenty of evidence that there was a seamy side to the patriotism of the gentlemen of England in Tudor times.

These gentry wanted watching but of course they had to be employed. According to most text-books, successful governments throughout history indulge in a process known as " centralisation ". Until very modern times this in fact has very seldom occurred. Quite certainly it was not what made Tudor government successful. The Tudors did not " centralise " their government. That is to say, they set up no " prefects " or " intendants " and made no attempt to run the whole country from " Whitehall ". They could not afford it and the state of the roads did not allow it. It might take a week or more for a horseman to get from London to Penzance or to Newcastle. No wonder, when a Spanish treasure ship was brought into Dartmouth, that Ralegh (who was out of favour and actually in prison at the time) had to be released and sent to secure the queen's share of the prize, since he alone could manage the wild Western men. The great Elizabethan traveller and antiquary William Camden thought it quite a hazardous adventure to visit a remote country beyond the mountains, called Lancashire, " which I go unto (God speed me well) after a sort somewhat against my will. . . . But I will proceed, in hope that God's assistance, which hitherto hath been favourable unto me, will not now fail me."[18] We need not be surprised that Elizabeth's government should have had to turn a blind eye upon the prevalence of Catholicism in Lancashire.

If anything, Tudor government shows a tendency towards decentralisation. Not only were separate local, self sufficient replicas of the Council set up to govern the North, Wales and the West; but the great mass of day-to-day administration for the whole country was made the responsibility of the local magnate in his capacity as Justice of the Peace. This officer might be harassed with innumerable enquiries into the minutiae of sewerage or musters, of road-repair or recusancy, of subsidy-assessment or of wage-rates. He had to satisfy the government's inordinate thirst for information. The Vice-Chancellor of Cambridge University even had to report to the Council on whether or not the undergraduates of Christ's College had acted a seditious play. Yet the only centralisation was a centralisation of what might be called " intelligence ". The local authorities were not permanently overseen by any grand official sent down from London, although on occasion Thomas Cromwell might carry out a visitation of the monasteries or a government commission might pursue on the spot its enquiries into some local problem. The normal practice was for the government to work through the local, amateur authorities, even if it kept a finger carefully upon their pulses and even if it kept them very well informed of the policies they were expected to enforce. In a sense the government co-opted every trustworthy member of the ruling class. Indeed Henry VIII once considered making every man of substance take the Councillor's oath. The whole system has been aptly called " self-government at the king's command ".

There were obvious disadvantages in a system which involved an almost absolute dependence on the goodwill of the justice of the peace. But at least it saved a lot of money; and money was the most vital of all considerations, for Tudor governments were, in relation to their needs, exceedingly poor. In a very large measure they were dependent on the more or less fixed income of a feudal king. There were strong prejudices against new forms of taxation and indeed against direct taxation of any kind, except in rare emergencies. The well-to-do were grossly underassessed for such taxes as there were. The Crown was hard hit by the price-rise that was going on throughout the century; for kings and queens, with their fixed rents and dues, had not the same chances as other landlords or employers of exploiting the price-rise to their advantage. Nor was the Crown able to retain for long any considerable portion of the plunder taken from the Church. There can be no doubt that the sovereign obtained nothing like a fair share of the rapidly increasing national wealth. His expenses, however, were rising steeply. It was very necessary to appear " majestical " and keep up a great state. The work of government in every possible direction was steadily increasing. Wars were costing more and more. Even the small wars of Henry VIII cost more than three million pounds, and Elizabeth's, in spite of her economies, cost well over five million. We must remember that in the year of the Armada her total revenue from all sources, apart from loans, was £392,000.* It is not wholly surprising that Henry VIII debased the coinage nor that Elizabeth profiteered by selling muskets to her own troops. It is little wonder that every Tudor monarch had to borrow and that all except Henry VII left the Crown in debt.

Quite apart from any lack of material ways and means for governing, the Tudors were faced with long-standing prejudices against governmental interference in the affairs of the subject beyond certain traditional points. Even if it was agreed that the sovereign was the national leader in war and that he had the sole right to make war, he was not expected to go to war without consulting his magnates. Even if he was recognised as the fountain of justice, there were numerous traditional franchises and private jurisdictions which he was not supposed to regard with too jealous an eye. It was not so long, either, since the rich and powerful had tacitly assumed that the law would not be enforced over-rigidly against them. In 1411 a judge of one of the royal courts had laid an ambush with five hundred armed men against a personal enemy, and then solemnly pleaded that he did not know it was against the law. There were plenty of magnates surviving into Tudor times who would have adopted a similar line of argument if given the slightest opportunity.

In spite of the obvious bankruptcy both literal and moral of the feudal aristocrats, there was throughout the Tudor period a widespread feeling that the sovereign ought to consult only with his " natural counsellors ", the old nobility. The Tudors never quite attained full freedom to appoint whom they liked as their advisers. Even Elizabeth had for form's sake to keep on her Council one or two representa-

* Whatever " multiplier " we adopt to find the equivalent value of money in our own day, this cannot be made to appear a large figure for the national budget. But, as certain commodities cost no less than they do now, it is safer to use no standard " multiplier " at all.

tives of the oldest families. There were chronic popular complaints about the " villein blood " appearing at the Council table from the time of Empson and Dudley to the time of Walsingham and the Cecils.

There was prejudice too on the subject of the " blood royal ", and it was never universally recognised that the crown could rightfully belong to a *de facto* ruler lacking the best possible hereditary claim. So long as there were descendants of the Yorkist line still living, the White Rose never quite lost its power to prick. It was this weakness in their hereditary title which prevented the Tudors from pulling out all the stops when they proclaimed the divine right of kingship; for the doctrine is in esssence a doctrine of the succession, attaching only to the rightful heir. There was some resistance even to the Tudors' use of the new title " His Majesty " in lieu of the older and less grandiose " His Grace ".*

" Majesty " was perhaps the quality which the Tudor sovereigns most pre-eminently possessed. The word, however, needs careful definition. It implies that the king is different in kind, not merely in degree, from the most exalted of his subjects; that he is no longer *primus inter pares* like a feudal overlord; that he lives in a high world of his own, in touch with certain mysteries of state which subjects cannot fully understand. " His ceremonies laid by ", the king may be " but a man ". The Tudors very seldom laid their ceremonies by. It was of set policy that they kept up the most elaborate and artificial pomp and splendour. They made a deliberate cult of the royal " Progress " and, for all their parsimony, neither Henry VII

* In Heywood's play *Edward IV* (*circa* 1599) an engaging character called the Tanner of Tamworth, a plain blunt man, meets the king in disguise.

" KING : The king is hunting hereabouts. Didst thou see His Majesty?
TANNER : His Majesty? What's that? His horse or his mare?
KING : Tush ! I mean His Grace."

nor Elizabeth economised on the outward trappings of majesty. A Tudor monarch could be undignified or even frivolous but none of them would allow the taking of any real liberty, just as a cat may suddenly scratch you in its play if you have gone too far. At the heart of every Tudor sovereign was something cold, aloof, detached, secretive. The bonhomie they sometimes showed was fundamentally false. And always they made it clear that they had to wrestle, in private and alone, with problems too deep and subtle for ordinary men. Henry VII showed it in his furtive and complex national housekeeping. Henry VIII really believed perhaps with some justice—that he understood theology better than his bishops, and amended their theological pronouncements when they had left loose ends : and when his matrimonial problem was called " The King's Great Matter " the implication was that it was a problem too deep for lesser men. Elizabeth's tortuous diplomacy threw off all pursuers, including her own foreign ministers.

The Tudors indeed kept their own counsel. No minister, not even Wolsey or Burghley, can ever have felt certain that he had the royal confidence. Nor could any minister feel properly secure, knowing that he could lose in a moment the royal favour and, with it, all protection from his enemies : and round the falling or fallen favourite the vultures would very quickly gather.

One feature of Tudor policy which served to emphasise the " majesty " of the sovereign was the dynastic marriage which the Tudors generally sought and sometimes obtained. In the previous century Henry IV, Edward IV and Richard III had taken wives from among their own subjects, but Henry VII betrothed or married his four children to foreign kings or princesses. One of his daughters, the Princess Mary, was later to incur her brother's anger when, without his leave, she got herself re-married to a mere English noble. Henry VIII married two princesses and paid suit to a third. The hand of Mary Stuart was sought for Edward

T.   B

VI. Mary Tudor was married to a reigning sovereign and Elizabeth allowed herself to be courted more than half seriously by at least four royal personages.

Nor was the popularity of the Tudors of the same kind as that attaching to popular kings of the preceding hundred years. Edward III, Henry V and Edward IV had all endeared themselves to their people by doing well those things which the nobility also liked doing, in particular by winning battles. Edward IV's very open lasciviousness detracted from the royal dignity, though not from his popularity; and the fact that his principal mistress was both a mercer's daughter and a goldsmith's wife seemed to the people to make the king very much one of themselves. The popularity of a successful Plantagenet somewhat resembled that of a successful captain of the eleven, whereas the popularity of a Tudor was more that of an effective headmaster.

The watch which the Tudors kept over England was inevitably a lonely vigil. The coldness and aloofness necessary to their success as rulers kept them from the warmth of human intimacy. Henry VIII did—perhaps twice—marry for love and each time the marriage had a tragic ending. Mary's marriage also was a personal tragedy. Elizabeth's virginity was a matter of policy, not of choice, and it took its toll upon her emotional life. The Tudors were not a happy family and the outward gaiety of Henry VIII or Elizabeth must often have been forced or hollow. Nor could any Tudor escape gnawing anxiety and neurosis, and a Tudor crown was indeed "polished perturbation, golden care". No Tudor sovereign was free from actual physical danger, since each had to deal with armed rebellion or invasion or with assassination plots. None could have felt sure of dying in their beds; still less could they have felt sure that their successor would carry out any of the projects which they cared for. Nor must we forget the *damnosa haereditas*, which is positively Aeschylean, of their family history—Mary's embittered youth and Elizabeth's knowledge that her own father had killed her mother. Incidentally, the mere weight of learning inflicted on a Tudor child must in itself have imposed no inconsiderable strain. His school-masters should perhaps share with his doctors the responsibility for Edward VI's death before his sixteenth birthday.

The Tudors paid a high price for their power. They were often unhappy and much of their unhappiness was expressed in inhumanity and visited upon their subjects, often upon the most devoted of their ministers. Empson and Dudley, Wolsey and Cromwell, were ill-rewarded for their services. So, of course, was Thomas More. Sir William Stanley won Bosworth for Henry VII but this did not save him from the block : and it was Henry VIII's death and not his gratitude which saved the life of Norfolk, who had once fought at Flodden. In order that the king's head should lie a little less uneasy the innocent descendants of the House of York were ruthlessly wiped out. Mary tried moderation for a time and then, maddened by frustration and despair, set alight the fires of Smithfield. Elizabeth might hesitate to execute the Queen of Scots for fear of all the repercussions; but she did not hesitate to hound on her lieutenants to see that enough poor men were hanged after the rising in the North. No village, she said, was to be without at least one execution.

Yet, even in their vices and their weaknesses, the Tudors did the state some service. The realm profited from Henry VII's sly, cold, ruthless, unromantic efficiency; for it needed retrenchment; it needed peace and order; and its hotheads needed cooling. Even the arrogance, the selfishness, the cruelty of Henry VIII served some useful purposes. In snapping his fingers at all the decencies of Christendom, in defying the great powers and calling the Pope's bluff, he taught his subjects that they too had some right to swagger, that they were citizens of no mean city, that " this realm of England is an Empire " which could stand on her own feet against the three corners of the world. Even the pathetic weakness of the boy Edward taught a salutary lesson; for it showed the country what it had owed to Henry VIII.

Henry had been selfish but he had been strong; and selfishness in the sovereign, provided he was also strong, was now seen to be more tolerable than the unrestrained ambitions of selfish oligarchs. The reign of Edward proved that there were wild men in the new society whose energies needed harness and discipline as much as the old robber barons'. Mary's fanaticism brought to light and strengthened a growing decent, moderate public opinion that respected the courage of the martyr and was shocked at the wanton persecution of humble, harmless, conscientious men and women. At the same time the Spanish marriage and the subordination of England's interests to Spain's disclosed a patriotic pride in Englishmen which could not brook humiliation. Protestant and Catholic excesses in turn helped to produce a demand for moderation. Thus even the two unsuccessful Tudors provided important object lessons for their people.

Elizabeth, the most successful Tudor, owed as much, paradoxically, to her feminine weakness as she did to her masculine strength. Her flirtations are unaesthetic but they had their diplomatic uses. Her vanity helped to make her an emotional focus for her subjects' loyalty. Her caprices prevented the growth of any over-confidence in potentially dangerous favourites or magnates, and kept hostile powers in the dark as to her real intentions. Her parsimony, even if it kept the national armaments at a dangerously low level, was of some assistance in avoiding national bankruptcy at a time of grave economic strain. Her evasiveness, though it shirked or begged many questions, at least delayed the coming of any real " showdown " with the Puritans or with Parliament. Her vacillation and her neurotic fear of irrevocable decisions happened, by sheer luck, to be in the national interest; for in many spheres and on many occasions in her reign almost any decision would in fact have been wrong; and, as it happened, what the country needed more than all else was time. Elizabeth was very great but also very fortunate and she builded better than she knew.

Tudor England was indeed a fortunate isle. It is not always realised how much she owed to sheer good luck nor how much the odds must have seemed to be against her attaining to any kind of greatness. She started a long way behind France and Spain politically, and a very long way behind Italy in all the arts. Her aristocracy was effete and irresponsible. Her rulers were usurpers, and her succession problem was never solved. Two Tudor sovereigns were females, and England had seen no queen regnant for the last four hundred years. It was indeed to remain doubtful until well on in Elizabeth's reign whether the state could survive at all with a woman on the throne. Tudor England was not a first-class power; her armies won no victories except against the Scots. Her economy was not stable. And, although the Armada was soundly defeated before the storm blew up and shattered it, the Spaniards certainly contributed to their own defeat. If Parma could have landed and kept open his supply line, his infantry must have won the war.

Nor was this the only occasion when England's enemies threw their chance away. Better leadership of the Pilgrimage of Grace, with some support from Charles V, would almost certainly have overthrown Henry VIII. If the Pope had moved against Elizabeth before she was established on her throne, and if he had prevailed on France and Spain to make common cause against her, it is difficult to see how she could have ridden out the storm. As late as 1569 the issue was still very much in doubt, for the Rising in the North was probably the most dangerous of the many crises of the century. That the Rising had good prospects may be judged from the fact that Leicester considered joining it. Even two years before the Queen's death the hare-brained Essex could still attempt armed rebellion in the streets of London. Yet, for all the slender forces at their disposal, the Tudors survived. They were clever; they were effective; they were courageous. But they were also exceedingly, almost miraculously fortunate. How, without such fortune, could their kingdom have succeeded in defying the threats and frowns of Catholic Europe? Perhaps, had England been more feared and less despised she would not have been allowed to survive. It was no less fortuitous and no less fortunate that the country should have come through so much political, social and religious revolution with so astonishingly little bloodshed. We know the price paid for such things in other parts of sixteenth-century Europe.

Fortune, without any doubt, smiled on Tudor England : but the smile was not wholly undeserved. Something, undeniably, was owed to the balance, the sanity, the moderation and the courage of the English people; and, not least, something to the personal magnetism, to the craft, to the coolness, to the judgment, to the sensibility, to the sheer strength of character possessed by a supremely gifted dynasty. The luck went to the cunning and fortune favoured the brave.

More was at stake than the mere survival of one particular royal family, for the collapse of the Tudors would certainly have meant the collapse of their realm. Even in 1603 there was some doubt as to whether James I and VI would succeed peacefully to his new throne. If the Tudors had fallen at any time before the execution of Mary Stuart and the defeat of the Armada, England would almost inevitably have subsided into wholesale anarchy and would at best have become a satellite of France or Spain. England would then have had to be rescued, if she was to be rescued at all, by a true dictatorship far more ruthless than the so-called Tudor despotism. British liberty might well have been still-born or strangled at its birth, since freedom is in so large a measure a by-product of political security. A different social structure must have resulted and the English country gentleman might never have attained to social or political power. It is unlikely that either Virginia or the East India Company would have been founded, and less likely still that England would have become what she was to be within a hundred years of the death of Elizabeth, namely, the wealthiest country in the world. The future of the Protestant religion must have become, to say the least, precarious; for it is doubtful whether the Dutchmen and the Swedes alone could have withstood the repeated onsets of the Counter-Reformation.

Imagination must boggle at the attempt to conceive the character of an England that was not a first-class power, possibly not even a united nor an independent realm, nor yet a land of political liberty; an England without squires and without colonies; an England shorn of nearly all her trade and wealth; an England that was not Protestant, still less Puritanical.

It is obvious that Milton would have died mute and inglorious and that Milton's England would not have been " a puissant nation " " shaking her invincible locks " or " mewing her mighty youth ". But what about Shakespeare? He was not particularly Protestant and certainly not a champion of political liberty. How far, if at all, was Shakespeare's achievement bound up with the political success of Queen Elizabeth? Great poets have flourished in Catholic countries, in states that were neither politically strong nor politically secure, in states without independence and without liberty; though perhaps less often in states without wealth, for poetry is on the whole a luxury product. Yet it is notable that Elizabethan poetry did not come to full flower until the end of the reign, the time when national self-confidence was growing so rapidly. It cannot be thought wholly accidental that Marathon and Salamis were followed so quickly by the works of Aeschylus and Sophocles. Patriotism, especially triumphant patriotism, can do much to focus and canalise the poet's wayward energies. Yeats found himself largely through the Easter Week rebellion. Did the Armada do the same thing for Shakespeare?

In any case, could a defeated England have afforded Shakespeare? He was not altogether cheap. He needed both patrons and an audience with some surplus wealth. There may be more than a rhetorical flourish in the words of a footnote to *A Treatise on Money* by the greatest economist of our time. " I offer it as a thesis for examination by those who like such generalisations, that by far the larger proportion of the world's greatest writers and artists have flourished in the atmosphere of buoyancy, exhilaration and the freedom from economic cares felt by the governing class, which is engendered by profit inflation."[19]

CHAPTER II

THE TUDOR HERITAGE

It is not often realised that the Wars of the Roses were very far from being a national disaster. Their destructiveness and continuity have been greatly exaggerated. They lasted for just over thirty years, but with long intervals including one of fourteen years. The armies engaged were very small and included a high proportion of foreign mercenaries, so that there was little effusion of English blood save that of factious nobles. It is true that a cavalry charge does not improve the crops and that wars and rumours of wars can be bad for trade and credit; but the fact remains that the period saw little intermission in the piling up of great fortunes on the part of wool merchants or in the building of expensive churches.

The government certainly was weak, except during the later years of the Yorkists; there were administrative breakdowns and considerable miscarriages of justice, since judges and juries were often corrupted or intimidated. Yet this had been so for the previous half-century and must not be attributed solely to the wars. The leaders of English society, even some of the most cultivated among them, were sometimes brutal and half-savage, like John Tiptoft, Earl of Worcester, who collected classical manuscripts but introduced the hitherto un-English habit of impaling his enemies. Tiptoft, however, shocked even his fellow-aristocrats and duly met with vengeance : he died bidding the executioner cut off his head in three strokes " as a courtesy to the Holy Trinity ". Caxton's preface to Malory's *Morte d'Arthur* (1485) informs the reader that the book is designed to see " that we fall not through vice and sin but exercise and follow virtue "; and therefore it describes " renowned acts of humanity, gentleness and chivalry ". The reader is not told that the author wrote it during a term of imprisonment for robbery with violence, attempted murder, sacrilege, extortion, cattle-raiding and "felonious rape". But perhaps the real moral of the story is that Malory did get imprisoned and was twice refused a pardon by King Edward IV.[1]

The wars themselves were not conducted with unusual rapine. Certainly the English countryside suffered nothing approaching the horrors undergone by France during the Hundred Years War. At Northampton in 1460 "the Earls of March and Warwick let cry through the fields that no man should lay hand upon the king nor upon the common people but only on the lords, knights and squires : then the trumpets blew up and both hosts countered and fought together half an hour ".[2] Other battles may have been less well conducted and such orders may not always have been carried out. Yet it is most unlikely that Shakespeare's picture of the carnage has any close relation to the truth. The son who had killed his father and the father who had killed his son, in *Henry VI, Part III,* are examples of extreme poetic licence. Shakespeare of course was writing Tudor propaganda; and it paid the Tudors to have the Wars of the Roses represented as a sheer hell on earth, so that restive subjects could be told : " Look what we have saved you from."

Some historians, relying admittedly on a more contemporary source, have based too much upon the *Paston Letters.* These do contain evidence of a great deal of disorder; but it so happens that the Pastons and their friends were closely concerned in the wars and lived in Norfolk, an unusually stormy county. By contrast, the contemporary *Stonor Letters* contain as little reference to civil war as do the novels of Jane Austen to the great war with France : and the Stonors had dealings with many more counties than the Pastons.[3]

Of course the wars did some harm, but what is not often

realised is that they also did positive good. The class that poured out its blood and wealth was a selfish, barbaric, treacherous oligarchy, a foreign ruling class who had contributed almost nothing to the welfare of mediaeval England. At the Norman Conquest they had virtually destroyed the highest Christian civilisation west of Constantinople. They had occasionally prevented a bad king from misgoverning but they had done more to prevent good kings from governing. They had wasted the country's substance in numerous foreign wars which did England little good beyond replenishing the barons' cellars with French wine. The war-lords had seldom even won their battles except during the short period when they had unleashed against the chivalry of France a new and terrible secret weapon, the English agricultural labourer with his long bow.

It was several centuries before the ruling caste troubled to learn their tenants' language. Edward III is thought to have been the first post-Conquest king who could speak a little English (with the possible exception of Henry I), Richard II the first to have had it for his mother-tongue, and Henry V the first to use it for military despatches. At the dissolution of the monasteries, the nuns of Lacock Abbey were found to be speaking Norman French. Nunneries, it must be remembered, had by then become largely a way of providing for the less eligible daughters of the well-to-do. English did not become the official language of the law courts until the reign of Henry VII; and for long afterwards lawyers continued to make notes and glosses in a most peculiar *lingua franca*, so that we may read as late as 1688 that " Richardson Ch. Just. de C. Banc ad Assizes at Salisbury in Summer 1631 fuit assault per prisoner la condemne pur felony que puis son condemnation ject un Brickbat a le dit Justice que narrowly mist, & pur ceo . . . son dexter manus ampute & fix al Gibbet sur que luy mesme immediatment hange in presence de Court."[4]

England had not taken a prominent place in the develop-

ment of culture during the high Middle Ages. Her medi-
aeval poems do not rival the greatest Latin hymns nor
the best Provençal lyrics. Durham is not Vézelay and
Salisbury is not Chartres. The great Saxon tradition of
illuminating, which had risen so high with the Lindisfarne
Gospels, petered out soon after the Winchester Bible. Many
English Scholastics, like John of Salisbury and William of
Ockham, did their best work abroad. In terms of culture,
Plantagenet England had been a second-class power and a
satellite power deriving most of her ideas from abroad.
Saxon England had exported Christianity to the Germans,
education to the Court of Charlemagne and works of art
even to Italy, where Saxon craftsmanship was highly prized.
Saxon art, too, was largely indigenous or at least stamped
its borrowings with a clear mark of its own. The arts of
later mediaeval England, though by no means negligible,
were much more plainly second-hand. Perpendicular architecture, it is true, was a superb achievement and a native
one, so that the early Tudors in their search for magnificence were safe enough in employing English masons. But
they had to import Flemish glaziers, Italian carvers and
Germanic painters to clothe the architectural bones. The
English craftsmen had obstinately gone on being Gothic;
and therefore, for the new " Renaissance " motifs, the
first two Tudors, whose taste was " Renaissance ", had to
look abroad.

For half the Tudor period English culture had little con-
fidence in itself and continued to imitate the foreigner.
English sonneteers went on toiling in the wake of Petrarch.
Even the leading English lawyers were sometimes oblivious
of the merits of English law and looked hopefully for a
" reception " of the Roman code. Only in music did the
English strike out on their own, with Taverner, Marbeck,
Tallis and Tye treading not unworthily in the steps of
Dunstable. But Henry VIII's severance of relations with
Catholic Europe was to have wide repercussions and did

much eventually to throw England upon her own cultural resources.

The story, however, can be traced farther back, for the greatest single cause of the cultural emancipation of England had really been the Wars of the Roses. The old aristocracy that went down in the wars had been a foreign aristocracy, while the new aristocracy that was coming up was English, bearing English names and drawing its wealth and strength largely from English wool and cloth. For good or ill, the new leaders of society did not look so much across the Channel. In some ways they were insular, provincial, philistine. Yet, although a nation's culture can profit from cross-fertilisation and from the interchange of ideas, it benefits no less from independence and self-confidence, from being well-rooted in its own soil, from taking the shape given to it by native instincts and traditions. It may be that the secret of Elizabethan England lies in her having been, for the first time since the Norman Conquest, " mere English " like her queen. It may be that the greatest contribution of the Tudors to their country's history was the release of the native energies of a people too long held subject to foreign influence and foreign rulers.

The extent to which the Wars of the Roses actually wiped out the old families has been exaggerated. It is true that fifty-three peers had attended the last parliament before the wars (1454), whereas only eighteen came to the first parliament of Henry VII. But some of the absent peers had been attainted and were to receive subsequent pardons, a few (from the North) were not summoned, while others were minors who in due course grew up and took their seats. What is more important is that the old feudal peerage had lost a great deal of its wealth and more still of its influence and prestige. And there were certainly some missing names. In the famous words of a later Chief Justice, Sir Ranulph Crewe, " Where is Bohun? Where's Mowbray? Where's Mortimer? . . . Nay, which is more, and most of all, where is Plantagenet? They are intombed in the urns and sepulchres of mortality."[5]

The Tudors were slow to create new peerages—even when the passage of a government bill through the House of Lords was uncertain. They remembered that a peer could be a nuisance and they retained the old belief that a peer should be someone really grand. Henry VII created only five new peers, and when he died there was only one duke in England. Henry VIII created thirty-seven peers but, of these, some seventeen date from the last eight years of his reign; and he followed Tarquin in lopping the heads of the tallest poppies and attainted two of his four dukes.* Elizabeth's new creations did little more than fill the gaps made by peerages that fell into extinction. By 1572 the only two existing dukedoms had both been suspended through attainder.† Nevertheless new names of some importance in the annals of England were added by the Tudors to the roll of peers—names such as Cecil, Dudley, Russell, Sidney, Sackville, Wentworth, Wriothesley, Paget, Cavendish. Two other names, Howard and Herbert, must have seemed almost *parvenus* in Tudor times, since neither had been ennobled before 1460. It is significant that all the new names are English,‡ whereas half of the surviving older houses had names like Bourchier or Courtenay, Devereux or de Vere. The English were beginning to run England.

The " new men ", however, did not get into the saddle all at once—in fact not completely nor finally until Henry VIII on his death-bed resigned himself to the inevitable completion of the revolution he had half-reluctantly begun.

* I exclude the dukedoms conferred on those of Catherine of Aragon's infant sons who survived for a few days; also the Duchy of Richmond given to Henry's bastard son.

† i.e. Norfolk and Somerset. No more dukedoms were created before Buckingham's in 1623.

‡ We need not take too seriously the claim of the Russells to descent from Normans called Roussel or de Rosel. See J. H. Round, *Peerage and Family History* (London, 1901), pp. 250-78.

He nominated a Regency Council of sixteen for the boy Edward, and they included no noble with a title more than twelve years old.

The Tudors were indeed reluctant and scarcely conscious revolutionaries. The reasons are many. Serious risks were involved in introducing any rapid or drastic or unpopular changes. The ruling house was always forced to feel its way, to move by careful stages after careful preparation. The sovereigns themselves had conservative sympathies in many matters. Above all, the revolution had really begun long before. The " new men ", the " new learning ", the " new religion ", the " new monarchy " were all deeply rooted in the past.

" The rise of the middle classes " has long since, through being overworked, become a virtually meaningless phrase; and, if it has a meaning, it is the merest truism. The middle classes have been rising during all but perhaps five hundred of the five thousand years of recorded history. A middle class, particularly in England, can now be traced much farther back into feudal times than was at one time thought possible. Feudal England had never been without towns or without trade; and therefore there had always been a burgher class. This class had gained much in social prestige through being able to recruit itself from the younger sons of nobles—a process which had quickened after the thirteenth century, during which primogeniture had become almost universally adopted in this country. As a result England had no rigid distinction between noble and non-noble or between land-owning and trading families. Nor was it by any means beneath a noble's dignity to be in some sense a business man. A number of fifteenth-century nobles made fortunes by lending money at very high rates to the king, while some business men, like the de la Poles and the Pulteneys, had already founded noble houses by the end of the fourteenth century through financing the king's wars.

The growth of trade had involved the growth of wealth—

not only for the exceptional big business man such as Dick Whittington but for innumerable thriving bourgeois families. A silent social revolution was to be brought about by the rise of comfortable middle-class households. The centres of social life had once been the parish church and the monastery (which was also a public hostel) and the great noble's hall. All of these had been very public places and the life in them a very communal life. The old noble household was to survive well into Shakespeare's day, when great ladies like Olivia could find too little privacy among so many hangers-on and poor relations. In fact, many a Tudor noble was to ruin himself by trying to keep up the old kind of " state " and a quasi-feudal retinue beyond his means. But alongside this, the smaller private house with its close family circle was growing up. Sir Thomas More's at Chelsea is one of which we have some inside knowledge, although perhaps the households of the Capulets or of the Merry Wives of Windsor—Shakespeare's only bourgeois interiors —are known to us more intimately still. It has been held that the growth of this home life fostered a new kind of personal or family religion and brought about a decline in the importance attached to sacramental, corporate worship as well as to the monastic ideal.[6]

The new attitudes to life conventionally associated with " the Renaissance " have a much longer history than was at one time supposed. There were successive classical revivals during the Middle Ages, notably the great rediscovery of Aristotle in the twelfth century. Virgil, Ovid and Cicero had had a continuous influence and popularity. Even Greek scholarship had never wholly disappeared from the West. Nor was " Humanism " unknown to the later Middle Ages, if by " Humanism " we mean belief in man's reason or belief that this world is not solely a source of temptation and a vale of tears.

The Scholastic philosophers were in a sense the greatest and purest of all rationalists. They claimed to have demonstrated most of the truths of the Christian revelation by the exercise of syllogistic logic. Man's reason, they held, was not only to be trusted but could ascend unaided to the highest of the eternal verities. The Schoolmen have been accused, not altogether unjustly, of trying to spin the whole universe out of their own minds. They rationalised, indeed, to excess, assuming that all known facts could be rationally explained, justified, reduced to order or given significance. There were to be no " brute ", untidy facts without a meaning— hence the mediaeval philosopher's resort to allegory when he found himself in a tight corner. If, for instance, the gospel says that the miraculous draught of fishes produced 153 fish, the fact must have some meaning. It can only signify the square of the apostles (144) plus the square of the Trinity (9).

Just as the powers of the human mind became thus exalted, so did the place assigned to human, mundane life in the universal scheme. St Francis and the friars proved that the Christian life could be led without fleeing from the world, by staying in the world and going about in it doing good. They were also capable of praising God for the beauty of " Brother Sun " and " Sister Moon " and even for " Our Sister Mother Earth which sustains and hath us in rule, and produces divers fruits with coloured flowers and herbs."[7] St Thomas Aquinas, himself a friar, said something no less new in arguing that God's Grace should not be thought of as " taking away nature " but rather as completing or supplementing nature, that the secular life could and should be lived for its own sake and had a value of its own.

The world became less closely associated with the Devil. By the later Middle Ages the state and the city had both acquired a notable existence; and it had to be admitted that men could serve God in the life of the citizen as well as in the life of the recluse. Religion, too, was gradually becoming more personal and less institutional. It was recognised that laymen could attain the beatific vision : There arose a great line of mystics, some of them laymen, and some of them women, like Juliana of Norwich—and not a few of them unorthodox, like Margery Kempe. Religious feeling was also growing in some degree less austere. There came to be more emphasis on God's mercy and less on God's judgement,* and a new interest in the human life of Christ. It is possible that the growth of devotional fervour centred on His Mother corresponds with the growing importance of family life and domesticity. Moreover, the high place accorded to woman in Renaissance society was, in a sense, foreshadowed by her idealisation in the late mediaeval world of chivalry.

Religious art had become less bleak and severe, laying less emphasis on the remoteness and ineffability of God. Charming landscapes appeared in the background of religious paintings, and graphic touches drawn from ordinary human life. It has been suggested that the growth of towns had led men to discover the beauty of the countryside, for a peasant has no leisure or inclination to admire physical nature. The fields are his factory, from which he wrests a precarious living, and are therefore not romantic, whereas a townsman may see them with new eyes.

Nor had the mediaeval world been lacking in the power of self-criticism. The history of monasticism is a long history of monastic reform. There is mordant satire in Dante and in Langland. Few sixteenth-century writers were to be more anti-clerical than Wyclif; and no sixteenth-century writer was more radically secularist or Erastian than Marsiglio of Padua. Not even Hume was to be more destructive of the philosophical assumptions of his day than had been William of Ockham. As soon as secular literature written by laymen began to flourish, from Chaucer's day onwards, criticism of clerical shortcomings became one of its stock themes. This, however, must not be misinterpreted. As a rule the

* Even in the early twelfth century the great Cluniac Romanesque churches had displayed Christ's mercy falling upon all sorts and conditions of men in the blood streaming from His outstretched hands. (See Joan Evans, *Art in Medieval France* (Oxford, 1948), pp. 38-9.) Yet there was to be a setback when the Black Death renewed the emphasis on judgement.

monks were criticised for not living up to their own high ideals. The laity still accepted the monastic ideal as being the highest form of the Christian life. Sir Thomas More, who could be very critical, was still entirely orthodox on this point and at times wore a hair shirt himself. The idea that asceticism was a mistake, a misuse of human energy, that the highest Christian life could and should follow a domestic pattern, was an idea hardly to be found before Luther.

On the other hand the founding of non-monastic schools, like Winchester or Eton, may have implied that there was already some dissatisfaction with the current monastic education. Strangely enough, Henry IV, a close ally of the Church, and the deeply devout Henry VI had set a precedent for the kind of monastic reform which involved actual dissolution when they dissolved the alien priories, that is, the small cells in England belonging to foreign monasteries. Some of these cells were turned into the college livings which Henry VI gave to his foundations at Cambridge and at Eton.

There had been criticism, too, of the conventional political order. Sir John Fortescue's *Governance of England*, written in the time of Edward IV, ascribes all the ills of the day to " lack of governance " and calls for a monarchy that is financially secure, for the suppression of " over-mighty subjects ", for the employment of middle-class administrators—almost all the things which the Tudors were in fact to bring about. The Tudor " new monarchy "—the phrase was invented by John Richard Green in 1876— was not very new. In the first place, many of its practices had been anticipated by the Yorkist kings; for they had made use of bourgeois counsellors, improved the solvency of the Crown, and made some moves against baronial private armies and against corruption or intimidation in the law courts.

Neither Henry VII, nor Henry VIII for the first twenty years of his reign, invented any new instrument of government. The Justice of the Peace, the Council, even the "Star Chamber" had all existed for some time. All that happened was that the two Henries made more use and more effective use of the machinery that was already available. They took the established mediaeval constitution and they made it work, as other kings such as Edward I had done before them. The constitution had never been unworkable so long as a king had real strength of character, real ability, and real power to win co-operation from the ruling classes.

These were precisely the qualities which the two Henries had. They were aided, of course, by their usual good fortune. It so happened that the old ruling class was dying on its feet and that the new ruling class was not yet fully confident in itself. The "new men" still preferred to stand in the king's shadow and they instinctively followed the lead of monarchs as business-like as themselves, who possessed their own drive and efficiency, their own taste for wheels that actually went round. The business men had also the acumen to see that what feathered the monarch's nest would, directly or indirectly, bring feathers to their own.

CHAPTER III

HENRY THE SEVENTH

1485-1509

Bacon, with his usual insight, spoke of Henry VII as "a wonder for wise men". He implied that the king did not possess the qualities that would make him immediately attractive to shallow or unperceptive minds. Henry was a politician; and Bacon thought him a politician's politician in the sense that Spenser has been called a poet's poet. Only a man well-versed in the game of politics would appreciate fully the king's supreme technical accomplishment. At first sight there was nothing about him that was spectacular, dramatic, romantic or calculated to give him immediate popular appeal. He was the only adult sovereign for over a hundred years who acquired no nickname. He has not gone down in history as "Crookback" or "Bluff" or "Bloody" or "Good". He is also the only adult king between Edward I and Henry VIII about whom no Elizabethan or Jacobean dramatist wrote a play. And this in spite of the fact that his story is fundamentally dramatic, for no other ruler of England (save Oliver Cromwell) rose from such small beginnings; and no other monarch is so obviously the poor boy who "made good", the adventurer who really "arrived" and attained all his ends against all the odds.

The reasons for his apparent lack of colour are not far to seek. They lie partly in the nature of his highest merits. He was an extremely clever man, possibly the cleverest man who ever sat on the English throne. But the English do not like their kings to be too clever. It was one of the things they held against Richard II and against James I. Henry's genius was mainly a genius for cautious manoeuvre, for exact timing, for delicate negotiation, for weighing up an opponent or a subordinate, and not least, a genius for organisation. It was allied to great patience and great industry. He was a competent soldier, but always chose peace instead of war as being so much cheaper and so much safer. These are admirable and invaluable qualities for a political leader in troubled times. They would also constitute a compelling case for making a man director of a great industrial concern. But they do not make a king seem a dashing or a glamorous figure.

There are many other reasons also. There is less surviving evidence about the personal character of Henry than there is for the other Tudors. This is partly due to sheer chance and partly to the king's habit of never giving himself away. He was an only child and he had learnt very early to keep his own counsel and to trust no confidant. Throughout his life he seems to have had no intimate friends except possibly Cardinal Morton, who has left nothing in writing, and (curiously enough) de Puebla, the Spanish Ambassador, who played a double game and was not over-loyal to his own master. De Puebla's despatches, naturally, are steeped in diplomatic discretion and do not tell us all they might. The king therefore remains for us aloof and enigmatic.

The mask he wore was to some extent deliberately inhuman. He wished to be remote and incalculable; he wished to be more feared than loved. He could not afford to be generous without seeming to be weak. Yet Henry was generous to Lambert Simnel and, at first, to Perkin Warbeck, although ruthless and relentless enough in his treatment of Suffolk (the son of Edward IV's sister) who was kept in prison for years after being hunted all over Europe, and of Warwick (son of the Yorkist Duke of Clarence) who was executed after fourteen years in the Tower. There was no serious evidence of treason against either, although their blood made them a potential cause of treason in others. Nor is it quite certain that it was not Henry who killed " the Princes in the Tower ".

Yet the mask *was* a mask. The conventional picture of

the cold, calculating, thin-lipped, skinflint king will not quite do. He seems to have been genuinely religious, with "a singular devotion" to Our Lady; and we cannot be certain how much it was ostentation, how much a troubled conscience, and how much genuine piety which made him arrange for the saying of ten thousand masses for his soul. He was more than religious; he was superstitious. He treasured a leg of his favourite St George. He accepted all the mediaeval cosmos and its magical symbolism and lore. It is said that, in a moment of ill-temper, he ordered the hanging of all the mastiffs in England on the grounds that mastiffs would attack a lion, the king of beasts. Another story tells of a falcon executed for an assault upon an eagle. In the king's Privy Purse accounts there are records of payments made to astrologers and alchemists and to "a stranger of Perpignan that showed quintessentia".

Part of the paradox of Henry VII is the paradox of his age. The late fifteenth century was a strange twilight world, startling to us sometimes for its almost open cynicism and sometimes for its conventional piety. Somehow it has never quite got into focus in our minds and is apt to be dismissed by the meaningless formula "an age of transition"—as if any age were ever anything else. Earlier, more obviously "mediaeval" centuries are more easily understood, or at any rate more easily labelled. But the age of Henry VII remains in a half-light. At times we are apt to feel not only that we cannot answer our questions about it but that we are not even sure what questions we should like to ask.

It is partly a matter of documentation. We know the main facts, figures and events, but there is a singular dearth of inside information. There is little to tell us "how it struck a contemporary"; for the chronicles do not make illuminating comments and there are few letters and no memoirs to let us into the real secrets. Above all, there is practically no literature of an ideological kind to explain the theories, the patterns and the categories which framed men's thoughts.

The little we know suggests that there may have been a curious divorce between theory and practice. Only one theoretical book survives from the period, Edmund Dudley's *Tree of Commonwealth* (1509). Its author was Henry VII's unpopular and unscrupulous minister. It might be expected that his book would be a cynical, Machiavellian treatise on how to run an efficient state on rigorous " business " lines.* In fact it is a typically mediaeval allegory, full of pious, mediaeval commonplaces about the importance of " keeping troth ", and it pays the highest respect to the feudal nobility as being the " chivalry " of the realm.

Henry VII had a not dissimilar outlook. He seems to have had a love for all the pageantry and panoply of an outworn and fast-fading chivalric civilisation. The architectural memorials he left behind him are a blaze of heraldry. He held tournaments and indulged in pomps and " progresses " that were labyrinths of intricate and elaborate allegory and symbolism. It was he who put about the great myth of the Tudor double rose, symbolising the union of the Yorkist and Lancastrian houses and the healing of the nation's rift. Some historians have maintained that, although the Yorkists fought under the white rose, there is no evidence that the badge of the red rose was ever worn by a Lancastrian army. The red rose of Lancaster may in fact have been a Tudor fabrication born of Henry VII's love for symmetry and symbols.

It is notoriously dangerous to speak of national characteristics, and there is no more treacherous ground for the historian. Nevertheless it cannot be denied and it may be important that Henry Tudor was a Welshman. The fact may contain some part of the answer to his riddle. We have a little contemporary evidence as to what Tudor Welshmen were like or were thought to be like. Who was it that was a brave and efficient soldier and also a stickler for " the cere-

* Henry VIII, on coming to the throne, had put Dudley in prison in order to court popularity. The book was written in an attempt to regain the king's favour.

monies of the wars, and the cares of it, and the forms of
it?" Who was it that said "there is figures in all things"?
Who was it whose talk ran on romantic names like Alexander and Pompey the Great? It was Shakespeare's
Fluellen. Who was it that believed the heavens at his
nativity to have been full of signs and wonders, and boasted
that he was "not in the roll of common men", and held
that

> no woman's son
> Can trace me in the tedious ways of art
> And hold me pace in deep experiment?

Who was it that, for all his high romantic talk, knew well
enough the right moment to withdraw his support from a
losing side? It was Shakespeare's Glendower.

There are elements of truth in the popular belief that
Welshmen are apt to be a little " fey " and yet the possessors
of sharp eyes for the main chance, romantics with a curious
streak of realism, brave, stubborn, quick-tempered, moody,
passionate, and also somewhat devious and hard to understand.

Whether or not he owed it to his Welsh paternity and
upbringing, Henry Tudor had all these qualities. We know
that he was consciously, and perhaps romantically, aware
of being Welsh. Fourteen of the first twenty-eight years of
his life had been spent on Welsh soil. He rewarded Welsh
bards and kept St David's Day. He called his eldest son
after King Arthur. He used the red dragon of Cadwallader
as supporter for the royal arms and had flown it as the
royal standard on the field of Bosworth. In the great chapel
at King's College, Cambridge, which was finished out of
the bounty of King Henry's will, the dragon prances in all
the sculptured heraldry. It glows in crimson in the highest
and most central place of all, in the stupendous eastern
window just above the head of the crucified Saviour. The
founder king, Henry VI, had left instructions that the
chapel furnishings should be of an austere and simple
piety. Henry VII and Henry VIII made the chapel highly

secular and highly ornate. They made it a shrine not of Our Lady but of " the Tudor myth ". But the dragons are as prominent as the roses and show that the myth was largely a Welsh myth. In Tudor times it was never forgotten that the ruling dynasty was Celtic; and it has been proved that in Spenser's allegory the " faeries " are Welsh and the " Britons " merely English.[1]

There can be no doubt that Henry was not wholly grim, sour or saturnine. The legend that he was so is largely due to Bacon, whose portrait of the king is sharp enough in outline but is deliberately kept in black and white. " For his pleasures," wrote Bacon, " there is no news of them." But this is quite untrue. We know, from Henry's expenditure, a lot about his pleasures; and there is no ground for taking Bacon's view that Henry only pretended to enjoy them.

The king, like other Welshmen, was musical and he never travelled without some of his numerous minstrels, trumpeters, harpists and pipers. He paid money " for flutes in a case " (£3 10s.), " for a pair of organs " (£30), " for a lute for my Lady Mary " (13s. 4d.), " to four sackbuts for their wages " (£7), " to one that set the king's clavichords " (13s. 4d.), " to the Princess's string minstrels at Westminster " (£2), " to a woman that singeth with the fiddle " (2s.), " to the Welsh harper " (6s. 8d.), " to the child that playeth on the recorders " (£1), to William Newark and, again, to John Sudborough " for a song " (£1), even " to him that playeth upon the bagpipe " (10s.), or " to Watt the luter that played the fool " (13s. 4d.). Three and four-pence was paid both " to the trumpets that blow when the king comes over the water " and also " to the children for singing in the garden ".[2]

Henry was also a keen sportsman, hunting and hawking in the royal forests, jousting, shooting at the butts, watching cock-fights or bear-baiting, collecting a lion (£2 13s. 4d.) or a leopard (£13 6s. 8d.) for the Tower menagerie. He indulged modestly in gambling and staked sums ranging from 12s. to £9 on bets made over chess, dice, cards, archery and tennis. He once lost three shillings' worth of tennis balls while playing and must therefore have hit very hard or very wildly.

His amusements appear sometimes crude, sometimes naïve and sometimes exotic. There are numerous payments to "the waits", "the May games", or for "the king's bonfire" (10s.), to morrice dancers, to play-actors, "to a tumbler upon the rope" (3s. 4d.), "to one that joculed before the king" (10s.), "to Ringeley Abbot of Misrule" for a Twelfth Night entertainment (£5), for "the disguisings" (sums up to £34), "to the foolish Duke of Lancaster" (3s. 4d.), even "to one that gave the king cut papers" (10s.), or "to a fellow for eating of coals" (6s. 8d.), not to mention "the great woman of Flanders" (£2) and "the Scottish boy with the beard" (10s.). And there was "a little maiden that danceth". She was paid at various times £1, £12 and £30. The discrepancies and the sums are startling but it might be unsafe to draw too strong an inference.

The picture that emerges is that of a king who was not without his gaieties nor without certain extravagances. He does not seem altogether a miser; and he cannot have been wholly morose and unapproachable. He rewarded quite generously all kinds of people who brought him all kinds of presents great and small. We find him paying "a mariner that brought an eagle" (6s. 8d.), "Clement for a nightingale" (£1), "for making of a bird's cage" (£2 4s. 6d.), "to Savage's wife for a partridge nest" (6s. 8d.), "to a woman for a nest of leverets" (3s. 4d.), "for a fresh sturgeon" (13s. 4d.), "to one that brought great carps" (1s. 8d.), "to Portingales [Portuguese] that brought popinjays and cats of the mountain" (£5). On his progresses the king unbent at intervals to scatter largesse. For "beer drunken at the farmer's house" (1s.), "to a poor man that had his corn eaten by the king's deer beside Woking" (3s. 4d.), to poor women for cherries and strawberries (1s.

8d.), "for acqua vitae" (5s.), for "two glasses of water"
(5s.), "for a red rose" (2s.), for "posies" (3s. 4d.), or even
"to a woman that clarified deer's suet" (3s. 4d.). "To a
man for a present of peascods" (3s. 4d.); "to the reapers in
the way in reward" (2d.); "to a little fellow of Shaftes-
bury" (£1). Henry appreciated herbs and spices and paid
5s. "for a pot of thyme", 6s. 8d. "for spices for hippocras"
and £17 5s. "to a Lombard for musk and amber".

Henry had other, most miscellaneous, tastes. He gave
8s. 6d. for a backgammon set, 13s. 4d. to "a priest that
made powder"—probably gunpowder—£3 6s. 8d. "to the
smith of Richmond for a little clock", 13s. 4d. for "a
glistening stone", 6s. 8d. "to Master Griffin the swimmer",
6s. 8d. "to a priest that wrestled at Cirencester", small
sums several times to "a Welsh rhymer" and £6 13s. 4d.
twice to "the rhymer of Scotland". This was almost certainly the reward of William Dunbar for writing "London,
thou art the flower of cities all". The king liked to see
men from remote countries. There were, for instance,
Knights of Rhodes, the "stranger of Constantinople"
(£6 3s. 4d.), the "Greek with a beard" (£1) and the "two
friars of Ind"—probably Franciscans—(£2). He spent
considerable sums on manuscripts and on printed books;
and he gave presents or pensions to "an Italian, a poet"
(£20) and to his laureate "the blind poet" Bernard André
of Toulouse, not to mention the payments "to Hampton
of Worcester for making of ballads" (£1) or to "my Lady
the King's Mother's poet" (£3 6s. 8d.).

Other revealing oddities can be found in the king's
expenditure. He could be generous to enemies, for he paid
£10 1s. for Richard III's tomb, and even £10 "to Sir
William Stanley at his execution"—possibly towards the
funeral expenses, possibly to provide a suitable guerdon for
the executioner. Then there was the 6s. 8d. paid "to the
heretic at Canterbury" whom the king himself converted,
although Henry was too insistent upon orthodoxy and upon
the due enforcement of law for the poor wretch to escape

burning. Henry's orthodoxy is also attested by a payment of £4000 "unto the Pope's use". He was a patron, too, of discovery and invention, for we find £10 (to be followed by later donations) given "to him that found the new isle", that is, Newfoundland. There were also 16s. 8d. "for a reward at the paper mill" and a slightly cryptic entry, "to Sir John Baptista maker of fumigation, £5".

Some of Henry's spending may seem unduly lavish. Between 1491 and 1505 he paid over £100,000 for jewellery; but jewels were a good investment. They were also a highly portable form of wealth, and the king may have remembered that he might one day be forced to pack in a hurry and flee his realm. In any case, outward magnificence yielded good political dividends since it emphasised the king's "majesty". His sumptuous banquets, with such delicacies as "lamprey in galantine", "peacock in hackle", "perch in jelly dipped", heraldic devices made of brawn or pastry and "castles of jelly in temple-wise made",[3] must be seen in the same light. But the item "to John Van Delf, for garnishing of a salad £38 1s. 4d." may seem excessive even for a foreign chef. Much the same can be said of the finery displayed in the royal clothing, such as "the king's hatband of silk" (4s.) or "an ostrich skin for a stomacher" (£1 4s.), not to mention the silk collars for the royal buckhounds.

Henry appears at his most and also at his least human in his matrimonial relationships and projects. Although he married for dynastic reasons, he seems to have been genuinely attached to Elizabeth of York. There is a touching account of how he hastened to comfort her when he was told of the death of their eldest son, Prince Arthur, and of how she in turn comforted him, reminding him "that God had left him yet a fair Prince, two fair Princesses; and that God is where He was, and that we are both young enough".[4]

On the other hand, as soon as Arthur was dead, Henry made indecent haste to negotiate the betrothal of his

younger son to Arthur's child-wife the Princess Catherine.
Even more indecently, he proposed at one time to marry her
himself—within a few weeks of losing his own queen. In
his negotiations with Catherine's father, Ferdinand of Aragon, Henry made the most shameless use of his trump
card, his bodily possession of the Princess. He kept her on
very short commons and even bullied the helpless girl into
writing to her father in favour of a match between Henry
and her own sister the widowed Juana of Castile. This
project was particularly sordid since Henry probably knew
that Juana's sanity was very doubtful. He may have supposed that Ferdinand was purposely exaggerating, for
diplomatic reasons, his accounts of her abnormality. She
was, after all, the greatest European heiress and Ferdinand
might well have been doubtful whether Henry was a
wealthy enough suitor. Henry pressed his suit regardless of
this, for some time; but eventually his ardour cooled when
he obtained incontrovertible evidence that the widowed
princess was in the habit of carrying with her everywhere
the embalmed corpse of her husband Philip of Burgundy.

Henry was widowed when he was forty-six. Men aged
more rapidly in Tudor times and there is some reason to
think that the king was already prematurely aged. Yet,
two years later, when he was thinking of marrying the
young widowed Queen of Naples, his enquiries about her
suggest appetites and interests not wholly appropriate to his
years and dignity. " If the king had been young," wrote
Bacon, " a man would have judged him to be amorous."
Henry required his envoys to satisfy him as to how much of
the queen's stature was due to high heels, how much she
owed to cosmetics, " to mark her breasts and paps whether
they be big or small ", " to mark whether there appear any
hair about her lips or not ", to discover how much she ate
and drank, and even " that they endeavour them to speak
with the said young queen fasting . . . and to approach as
near to her mouth as they honestly may, to the intent that
they may feel the condition of her breath, whether it be

sweet or not, and to mark . . . if they feel any savour of spices, rosewater or musk by her breath or not ".[5] And there was much more, on matters more usually mentioned, about her complexion, her hair, the colour of her eyes, the shape of her nose, her neck, her hands and fingers, her tastes and temperament. It was, of course, a less reticent age than our own and one in which princes had necessarily to conduct their wooing at a distance.

There are other difficulties which beset the path of a historian who tries to assess Henry VII's achievements. They were undoubtedly great but they are not spectacular, they are a little elusive, they are not always edifying and they are mainly negative. He avoided bankruptcy; he avoided disorder; he avoided war; he avoided national humiliation; above all, he avoided losing his throne. He had limited objectives but, as Bacon said, "what he minded he compassed ". Most of it was done by sheer hard work and by exploiting to the full what resources, economic and political, the king found ready to hand. It is partly the lack of any startling innovation which makes Henry's achievement appear colourless. He simply took the existing machinery and used it effectively.

There is, however, something almost spectacular about Henry's finance. The bare figures speak for themselves. He raised the income from crown lands from £13,633 to £32,630 and the customs revenue from about £20,000 to over £40,000.[6] For the first five years of his reign, Henry's income averaged £52,000; for his last five years it averaged £142,000. The Crown when he acquired it was heavily in debt, and for some years he had to borrow money; but by 1492 he had repaid all his loans and could show a surplus in the royal accounts. From 1497 onwards he was able to save really large annual sums and at his death he left a balance credibly estimated as something in the region of a million and a half pounds.[7]

All this was brought about by methods that sound simple enough but in fact involved the greatest resolution and the greatest finesse. He resumed crown lands that had been granted away by his weaker predecessors. He squeezed all that was possible out of his feudal rights. He cut down waste and carried out wholesale reorganisation in the government departments which ran his financial affairs. He enforced the law sternly against offenders, particularly rich offenders, and extorted maximum fines. He encouraged trade and saw that he got his rightful tolls from it. He bullied men into making him loans—or sometimes gifts. He remained almost permanently at peace and when he did go to war he saved more than half the money voted by parliament and clergy for his military expenses. He managed once (in 1492) to get parliament to grant him money for a war with France and then to extort more money from the King of France for not pursuing his intention.

One of the most striking and paradoxical of Henry's achievements lies in the fact that in 1489 the Earl of Northumberland, who had been for some months in the Tower and came of a long line of particularly turbulent " overmighty " subjects, was killed in a village riot at Topcliffe while collecting a royal tax.[8] Henry had shrewdly seen that the far North would obey none but a Percy. And the king had somehow appealed to the loyalty and to the interest of a great feudal magnate.

Sometimes, in order to raise money, the king stretched the law, and sometimes he ignored it. Sir William Capel, Lord Mayor of London, was once heavily mulcted for a highly technical illegality and later imprisoned for no offence other than refusing to pay Henry £2000 and saying that " the king had no authority in the City of London ". The father of Sir Thomas More went to the Tower for arguing in parliament against a grant to the king and was only let out on payment of £100. And there was the famous case of the Earl of Oxford who was fined £10,000 for entertaining the king too lavishly and with too many liveried retainers. Most of these occurrences fell within the last years of the reign when the king's affairs were in the hands of Empson and Dudley. But Bacon claimed to have seen an account book of Empson's in which every page was initialled or annotated in the king's own hand. It showed, Bacon thought, "a nearness" in the king "but yet with a kind of justice".

Justice the king certainly enforced, sometimes by high-handed methods. Juries were occasionally punished for bringing in the "wrong" verdict. It was a practice that seems outrageous to ourselves but it was often very necessary in Tudor times. There was no other way of combating bribery and intimidation. Henry's use of "Star Chamber" procedure was no less necessary and no less salutary. "Star Chamber" was only the name popularly given to the Council when it sat in a certain building in Westminster and turned its attention to judicial matters, in particular to the problem of the "over-mighty subject". The Council's judicial powers had on several earlier occasions been recognised by parliament and had, in a sense, existed before there was any parliament in England. The so-called "Star-Chamber Act" of 1487 was a highly "declaratory" act, calling attention to powers that were already legal and it may not have referred at all to the actual body that came to be known as "the Star Chamber".[9]

In constitutional matters Henry was no innovator. He did not even begin the co-operation between king and parliament that is usually associated with the Tudor monarchy. Indeed the House of Commons might well have atrophied as did the Spanish Cortes and the French Third Estate, if Henry VIII had not found parliament a convenient instrument with which to beat the Pope. That is why the great landmark in English constitutional history is 1529, the date of the meeting of the Reformation Parliament, rather than 1485. Henry VII used parliament less and less as his reign went on and as he came to feel more secure and less in need of allies, money or support. Seven parliaments met during the reign and sat for some ten and a half months out of the twenty-four years. The parliament of 1504 was Henry's only parliament during the last half of his reign. Significantly it was the parliament whic allowed the king to reverse attainders, which were acts of parliament, on his own initiative. He was also extremely careful not to allow parliament to make him king. His right to the throne was openly and almost cynically based on his being king *de facto*, not exactly by divine right but by act of God, by virtue of the victory at Bosworth. He argued simply that he was king because he could be seen wearing the crown, that possession was in this case all ten points of the law.

Henry's title by heredity was almost non-existent. His paternal grandfather had married Henry V's widow, after some years as her clerk of the wardrobe. Henry's mother, Margaret Beaufort, was descended from John of Gaunt by his mistress and, although a parliament had made the family legitimate, it had also expressly barred them from the throne. In any case, if Henry's claim came through his mother, it was she and not her son who should have succeeded to the throne. There were, at his accession, at least ten other persons with a better title than his own.

To have remained on the throne for twenty-four years, without serious civil war, and in spite of all the pretenders legitimate or illegitimate, was in itself no mean achievement. It was in fact Henry's greatest feat and it made possible all his others. He was able to restore England's prestige abroad only by convincing foreign monarchs of his own security. The country's financial and administrative recovery was also contingent upon freedom from further civil war. The people needed a period of uneventful but efficient and continuous government to make possible the exploration and exploitation of their own latent resources. Behind the scenes the foundations of a greater England were being quietly laid, and one of the numerous silent social revolutions of English history was taking place. Ocean-going ships and comfortable houses were being built. The justice of the peace was warming to his work. Books were being printed and being widely read. Travellers were going to Italy and returning with new ideas and new aesthetic tastes. Foreign scholars, artists and technicians were being welcomed in England. The clergy and the " old " scholastic learning were coming under desultory fire. New schools and colleges were being founded. Fortunes were being made from wool and cloth. London was growing very big and very prosperous. An observant Venetian diplomat, writing about 1497, thought England had already become the richest country in Europe, and he noted that " in one single street, named the Strand, leading to St Paul's, there are fifty-two goldsmith's shops, so rich and full of silver vessels, great and small, that in all the shops of Milan, Rome, Venice and Florence together, I do not think there would be found so many of the magnificence that is to be seen in London ".[10]

The same shrewd Italian also noticed that the English had become self-satisfied. They were " great lovers of them-selves. . . . They think that there are no other men than themselves and no other world but England; and whenever they see a handsome foreigner they say that ' he looks like an Englishman ', . . . and when they partake of any deli-cacy with a foreigner, they ask him ' whether such a thing is made in his own country '."[11] He found in the English many of the characteristics that are so often said to have come in with the Reformation. He found them formal, reserved, dour, avaricious, insular and gluttonous. And he had " never noticed one of them to be in love ".[12]

The Venetian saw, too, how much the English owed to their king, but he thought him more feared than loved, since the people " generally hate their present, but extol their dead, sovereigns ".[13] No English king, he said, had ever " reigned more peaceably " but he saw that this was not due to any lack of courage in the king. He also noted Henry's bulldog, Churchillian tenacity. " Heretofore, it has always been an understood thing that he who lost the day lost the kingdom also; but the present King Henry, in all his reverses, showed that, even were all the rest lost, he would defend himself in the fortresses ".[14]

The Venetian was wrong about one thing. He expected Henry, should he live ten years longer, to bring in many revolutionary changes. But Henry remained orthodox, conventional, conservative, to his dying day. He was, for instance, less anti-clerical than many of his subjects, although he did, in the interests of law and order, put a stop to the grosser abuses of sanctuary and of benefit of clergy. At the end of his life he was considering continental adventures in the traditional, mediaeval pattern; and he even talked fairly seriously of going on a crusade against the Turks. But it was symptomatic of his caution and perhaps of a sardonic humour that he made his going conditional upon two other sovereigns going with him. It may also be symptomatic of the new age he lived in that, when the hat was passed round his court on behalf of the crusade, the collection amounted to eleven guineas.

CHAPTER IV

HENRY THE EIGHTH

1509-1547

Like his father, in fact like every Tudor, Henry VIII presents the historian with a problem : but it is not the problem of his personality. There is a mass of evidence about that. It is the problem of his reign. Indeed, it poses many problems. Why did he do so little in the first half of his reign and so much in the second? What turned the easy-going, orthodox, conventional king into the tyrant and the revolutionary? Why was he always relatively popular? Why was he almost always able to get his own way? Above all, there is the problem of the English Reformation. Why did it happen and why did it succeed? And how much of it can be laid to the king's sole account?

Without doubt the young Henry had remarkable endowments. For many years he could easily sustain the part expected of an ideal king. He was a Renaissance " magnifico ". He had also an apparent touch of a more mediaeval gallantry. He could play the knight-errant and he could play the philosopher king. He was rich, splendid, vital, hearty, handsome, dashing, affable, ingratiating, athletic, musical, an accomplished linguist, a patron of the arts, orthodox, self-confident. He had charm and he had force of character. His extravagance could easily be taken for liberality after the parsimonious days of Henry VII. His throwing of Empson and Dudley to the wolves seemed to promise a more " constitutional " mode of governing. His execution of Suffolk in 1513 only suggested that he had the courage to pluck the last dangerous thorn from the white rose, and make the realm finally secure against renewed civil war.

Wolsey's secretary and biographer, George Cavendish, records that the new king was admired as " natural, young, lusty and courageous . . . entering into the flower of pleasant youth " and that, with him, the country was thought to have entered " a golden world ".[1] Perhaps Sir Thomas More put his finger on Henry's secret when he wrote to Fisher, " the King has a way of making every man feel that he is enjoying his special favour, just as the London wives pray before the image of Our Lady by the Tower till each of them believes it is smiling upon *her* ".[2] More did not think himself " a special favourite " but he in his turn was to be subjected to Henry's facile charm. Roper could remember the king calling unannounced at More's house in Chelsea " to be merry with him . . . and after dinner in a fair garden of his walked with him by the space of an hour holding his arm about his neck ".[3] More's own comment was " If my head could win him a castle in France . . . it should not fail to go ".

Henry's liberality had seemed boundless and genuine. Lord Mountjoy, one of the king's intimates, wrote to his friend Erasmus bidding him hurry back to England. " Avarice ", he says, " has fled the country. Our king is not after gold, or gems, or precious metals, but virtue, glory, immortality. . . . Just lately he was saying he wished he were more learned. 'That is not what we want from you, I said, 'but that you should foster and encourage learned men.' 'Why, of course,' he said, 'for without them life would hardly be life.' "[4] Erasmus hastened to England but received no office or bounty from the king, who found it cheaper to let the great scholar be supported—with a modest sinecure—by Archbishop Warham.

Mountjoy, as a courtier, may have flattered Henry but the Venetian Ambassadors are likely to have been more objective. It is true that Wolsey violated the immunity of the diplomatic bag and forced the Venetians to encipher their reports, but their cypher, though simple by modern standards, may well have been secure against Tudor crypto-

graphers.* Presumably then, what the Venetians say of
Henry need not be thought flattering.

Their accounts make a very complete picture. The king,
we hear (in 1519) " is extremely fond of tennis, at which
game it is the prettiest sight in the world to see him play,
his fair skin glowing through a shirt of the finest texture ".[5]
Four years earlier another Venetian had thought Henry the
" handsomest potentate I ever set eyes upon : above the
usual height, with an extremely fine calf to his leg, his
complexion very fair and light, with auburn hair . . . and a
round face so very beautiful that it would become a pretty
woman, his throat being rather long and thick ".[6] We hear
of his skill at jousting and at archery and of his musical
tastes and accomplishments. Henry had induced Dionysio
Memo, organist at St Mark's, Venice, to accept a chaplaincy
at the English court; and the king made one Venetian envoy
sit through a four-hour performance of Memo's works.[7] We
hear of the king's gorgeous clothing—one day " in stiff
brocade in the Hungarian fashion ", another " in white
damask in the Turkish fashion . . . all embroidered with
roses made of rubies and diamonds, in accordance with his
emblem, a most costly costume ".[8] Or again, we hear of him
accoutred for jousting, with ten noble attendants, all (men
and horses) in " cloth of gold with a raised pile " and the
king looking " like St George in person ".[9] On the other
hand when a proclamation had forbidden the English gentry
to wear silk, the king could set a new fashion by wearing
a " long grey cloth gown ".[10]

Some of the Venetians were perhaps over-susceptible to
Henry's charm. One envoy, whose health suffered from the
English climate, records that the king shed what the
ambassador supposed to be real tears on seeing his " hag-
gard appearance ".[11] Another describes Henry's generous

* It was a substitution cypher, with variants for the vowels, combined with code symbols for certain proper names, e.g. M for the
Emperor (Maximilian) and a crescent for the Grand Vizier,
although others are rather less transparent.

treatment of his French prisoners, halving their ransoms and
" saying to the captor ' I'll pay the rest.' "[12] Another seems
to have been persuaded of the king's apparently genuine
love of peace and to have believed Henry when he said,
" I am content with what I have; I wish only to govern my
own subjects." But the Venetian also records that Henry
went on to say, " Nevertheless I will not allow anyone to
have it in his power to govern me, nor will I ever suffer it."[13]
These prophetic words were spoken in 1516. The peace-
loving, uncovetous king, however, is also described by less
ingenuous Venetians as having designs to make himself
king of France, of Scotland, of part of Castile and even of
Jerusalem.[14]

The young king had brilliance, but his talents were ill-
disciplined and ill-directed. He attended to the business of
government only by fits and starts when the mood took him
and when the pursuit of pleasure allowed it. He found the
act of writing " tedious and painful ", a fact which makes his
copious letters to Anne Boleyn the more significant.[15] He
made slight illness a ready excuse for refusing to work for
days on end. Affairs of state might be shelved in favour of
a special matins in honour of the Virgin or even in favour of
his " harts and hounds ". And, if he was tired after hunting,
his ministers found it inadvisable to bother him with official
documents.[16] A Milanese ambassador records that in 1513
the king " put off our discussion to another time, as he
was then in a hurry to go and dine and dance afterwards.
In this he does wonders and leaps like a stag."[17] The
English mode of dancing was always an oddity to southern
Europeans, and, to one of Philip of Spain's attendants at
Mary's court, English ballroom technique was to seem
" not at all graceful " but to " consist simply of prancing
and trotting ".[18] In the *Faerie Queene* the Graces in their
dancing can be heard to " thump ".

Henry was not wholly frivolous. For one thing, he made
an intellectual hobby of theology. He was later to make his
own marginal comments on the doctrinal pronouncements

drawn up by his bishops; and his book against Luther in
1521 was almost all his own work. He tried afterwards to
maintain that More had exercised a guiding hand, but this
was untrue. More had only done some " sorting-out " when
the book was finished. Indeed it is one of the ironies of
history that More had urged the king to be cautious in his
exaltation of the Pope's authority, pointing out that the
Pope " is a prince as you are " and that " there may grow
breach of amity and war between you both. I think it best
therefore that . . . his authority be more slenderly touched
on. ' Nay,' quoth his Grace, ' that it shall not. We are so
much bounden to the See of Rome that we cannot do too
much honour to it '." And the king brushed aside More's
objection that by Edward III's Act of Praemunire " a good
part of the Pope's pastoral cure here was pared away ".
Henry replied, " We will set forth that authority to the
uttermost. For we received from that See our Crown Imperial "—a doctrine which, said More, " till his Grace with
his own mouth told it me, I never heard of before ".[19]

It is also notable that during the reigns of four consecutive
pontiffs Henry was always the Pope's ally, sometimes to the
national disadvantage. How then are we to account for the
breach between the Holy Father and this particularly
dutiful and devoted son? The king's own orthodoxy must
not deceive us. Improbable as any breach between Henry
and the Pope must have seemed before 1529, a breach
between the English nation and the Roman Church had
long been a genuine possibility.

The English were devout enough and impressed foreigners
by the regularity of their prayers and masses. The church
bells were seldom silent and caused England to be known
as " the ringing isle ". There was no falling off in ecclesiastical building, which continued unabated till the breach
with Rome. Bath Abbey and the tower at Fountains are
both early Tudor. So is the glass at Fairford and at
King's College, Cambridge. There was even a marked
increase in the habit of leaving money to endow masses

for testators' souls. The Earl of Oxford in 1509 arranged for the saying of two thousand masses, while Colet's father, a Lord Mayor of London, financed a daily mass to be said on his behalf by two priests for fifteen years. Colet himself may have thought his father's form of piety somewhat mechanical, since he did not provide for the saying of any masses for his own soul. Mechanical piety, though it might earn the scorn of the better educated, was indeed the vogue. On a visit to Coventry More found himself highly unpopular for trying to laugh away the tenets of a local fashionable preacher who held that a man could not be damned if he recited the rosary daily in the Virgin's honour.[20]

The cult of relics remained exceedingly popular. At Walsingham Erasmus was shown the milk of the Virgin in pristine liquescence and at Canterbury the bones of St Thomas with still-bleeding flesh attached, not to mention a handkerchief which retained the saintly sweat and nasal effluvia. In Old St Paul's there flourished the cult of the fictitious St Uncumber, a bearded virgin who could rid women of unwanted husbands in return for pecks of oats. And when Friar Forest was burned at Smithfield in 1538, the executioners threw on the fire a great wooden image of an armed warrior which eight men could scarcely carry. It had been " brought out of Wales " and was known as " Darvel Gatheren " and it was reputed to fetch damned souls out of hell. Behind it lay who knows what mysterious fusion of Christian with Druidic rites. Bishop Barlow called it " an antique gargoyle of idolatry ", and with good reason, for it was almost certainly Hu Gadern the Celtic god of war.[21]

Yet devotion, however fervent, did not necessarily make the people over-fond of clergymen. In 1515 Richard Hunne, a prosperous, popular and truculent London tailor, refused to surrender his dead baby's " bearing-cloth " (worth half a crown) as a mortuary fee to the officiating cleric. He lost his case in a church court and promptly sued the cleric in King's Bench for a breach of *praemunire* in making use of " a foreign tribunal ". Hunne was at once charged with heresy, put into an ecclesiastical prison, and, a few days later, was found hanging in his cell. After one look at the corpse, and at the state of the cell, the coroner's jury had no hesitation in deeming it murder by connivance of Dr Horsey, Chancellor of London. Fitzjames, the Bishop of London, asked Wolsey to set up a special committee of the Council to try the case, on the grounds that any jury of Londoners would convict any cleric " be he innocent as Abel; they be so maliciously set *in favorem haereticae pramitatis* ".[22]

Nor was it only in London that the clergy were unpopular. The peasantry murmured against tithe and occasionally resisted payment by resort to arms—under the command, they said, of their captain, Poverty.[23] Self-appointed spokesmen for the poor wrote pamphlets blaming all their troubles on the ecclesiastical idle rich. Lollardy, in a form which was mainly anti-clerical rather than doctrinal, still smouldered in several counties after more than a century of ruthless persecution. Pluralist and absentee ecclesiastics caused no little scandal, especially in really flagrant cases such as that of Wolsey's bastard son who held thirteen ecclesiastical offices while still a schoolboy. Four consecutive Bishops of Worcester were absentee Italians at least one of whom was a murderer. Wolsey was Archbishop of York for sixteen years before he entered his diocese and then did so only as a disgraced and dying man. Other bishops spent all their working lives in some civil administrative post; and several remained permanently overseas as ambassadors.

It is significant that things which might well have seemed scandalous were often taken as a matter of course even by critics and reformers and even by the most devout. Warham, for instance, only took priest's orders at the age of fifty-three in order to become a bishop. Even Colet had not become a deacon before the age of thirty, although he had already enjoyed the fruits of seven ecclesiastical offices.

Perhaps it did not become him over-well to denounce pluralism in quite the tone he did. The austere Pole, no less, had held two deaneries, two prebends and a rectory before he took deacon's orders at the age of thirty-eight. He was to be Archbishop-elect before he became a priest.[24]

Few of the higher clergy can be called very zealous, although there were honourable exceptions like Fisher and Fitzjames; and, even had their holders been more often present or more often saintly, the English dioceses were mostly too large to be efficiently controlled. On the eve of the Reformation, the Pope himself was on the point of sanctioning the dissolution of superfluous English monasteries to finance the founding of new sees. It may not be wholly accidental that the Reformation obtained a permanent hold only in those countries where episcopal sees had been very extensive.

With so little supervision, it was inevitable that the rank and file of the clergy should often have been ill-educated. In 1551 Bishop Hooper examined 249 clergy in his diocese of Gloucester and found that 171 could not say the ten commandments, 33 being ignorant of where to look them up : 10 could not repeat the Lord's Prayer, 30 did not know where it was to be found and 27 could not nominate its Author.[25] One of the most ignorant was a "doctor". It is by no means impossible to believe the story of the early Tudor vicar of Trumpington who paused in his reading of the lesson when he came to " Eli, Eli, Lama Sabachthani " and said to his churchwardens " ' Neighbours, this gear must be amended. Here is Eli twice in the book. I assure you if my Lord of Ely come this way and see it, he will have the book. Therefore by mine advice we shall scrape it out and put our own town's name " Trumpington, Trumpington, Lama Sabachthani " '. They consented and he did so, because he understood no Hebrew."[26]

Scandal, alleged or actual, about the clergy might not have mattered if the clergy had been less numerous, less wealthy, less prominent, less privileged, less powerful or less able to affect men's daily lives. But there was perhaps one clergyman for every fifty or a hundred laymen, compared with one for every fifteen hundred today. York is said to have had five hundred clergy among its ten thousand inhabitants.[27] The clergy may have controlled, directly or indirectly, at least a tenth of the whole national income and as much as a quarter of all English land. They occupied very many of the highest political and administrative posts. They were largely exempt from the jurisdiction of the civil courts, whereas their own courts could inflict penalties on laymen for numerous offences. Even the fine imposed on the cleric who begot a bastard (five shillings) was lighter than the two pounds which it cost the layman. The fine, known as a "cradle crown", was regarded as virtually the purchase of a licence, and bishops would often wink at such a convenient augmentation of their revenues.[28] The clergy could and did shut the butchers' shops for the seven weeks of Lent and on all other fast days. They made all laymen take communion and confess their sins at least once a year. They alone dealt with all wills and testaments and they took large mortuary fees. They could conduct much effective propaganda from the pulpit or, at times, in the confessional. And there was no appeal against a conviction for heresy in their courts.

We do not have to believe every scandalous story told about the clergy; and we should remember that the abuses of any institution are far more likely to attract attention than its better side. If an institution is working well, the fact will normally be taken for granted and few writers will trouble to record it. Yet abuses there were, without doubt, and it is notable that no new monastery had been founded in England since Syon Abbey in 1415,* while it was admitted on all hands that most monasteries on the eve of

* Apart from six houses of observant Franciscans founded between 1482 and 1507 mostly under the patronage of Henry VII. See M. C. Knowles, *The Religious Houses of England* (London, 1940), pp. 58, 111.

the dissolution were seriously undermanned. It would appear that the monastic ideal had been losing its attractions and that monasticism had begun to seem an anachronism which had outlived its usefulness. Foreign observers commented on the marked anti-clericalism of English laymen; and certainly Hunne's case had provoked anti-clerical storms in the Parliament of 1515. Benefit of clergy had already been modified and a number of the smaller monasteries dissolved long before the king began to have matrimonial troubles.

Besides, if ever Henry needed a precedent for dissolving a religious order which had become too independent or too rich for his liking, he could have cited the examples of Philip the Fair of France and of Pope Clement V who had, from pure greed and jealousy, dissolved the Templars with revolting brutality and singular injustice. Moreover, the alien priories of England had been dissolved, without any popular protest, by the king's most saintly predecessor, Henry VI.

Indeed it is probable that only Wolsey and his pious king stood between the clergy and the storm that might any day have broken over their heads. And the king himself had once, significantly, shown a claw when in 1515 Dr Henry Standish was attacked by his fellow clerics for supporting the case against benefit of clergy. The king, for all his orthodoxy, let fall a thunderbolt. " The Kings of England," he said, " in times past have never had any superior but God only. Wherefore know you well that we will maintain the right of our crown and of our temporal jurisdiction . . . in as ample a wise as any of our progenitors."[29]

There was anti-clericalism in other countries; but there were special reasons why in England it led to a formal breach with Rome. It is probable that the English were the most insular and nationalist of all the European peoples. It is possible that England had the strongest middle class and that the English government depended more than any other on middle-class support. And anti-clericalism was mainly a middle-class phenomenon. In England, moreover, papal power had come to mean the power of the Legate Thomas Wolsey who was hated not only by the nobles, the lawyers and the taxpayers, but by most of his own bishops. His wars and diplomacy, which had been expensive and inglorious, had almost all been either pro-papal or else intended to further his own designs on the papacy. Hatred of his power could and did slide easily into hatred for the Pope's. What the historian has to explain is not so much why there was a Reformation in England but why there was so little resistance to it; and in Wolsey it may well be thought that much of the explanation is to be found. For he epitomised not only the power of the Church but the patent worldly-mindedness of so many of its princes. It is unlikely that the Duke of Suffolk spoke for himself alone when he told Wolsey, " It was never merry in England whilst we had cardinals among us."[30]

Yet the king had long protected the cardinal and with him the Church against dukes, parliaments, heretics and all other enemies. Cardinal and Church may possibly have been doomed in any case; but they fell when they did because the king's emotions had passed into a new and stronger gravitational field. By the regal standards of his time, Henry cannot be thought unduly lascivious, and he is not known for certain to have formed more than two extramarital ties. But he was in the prime of life and his queen was six years his senior, with waning charms. All the same, it must remain somewhat surprising that sexual passion should have turned a conservative, easy-going, politically cautious ruler into a revolutionary, head-strong, almost reckless tyrant. Nothing else, however, will account for the facts.

In 1527 Henry wrote to Anne Boleyn that he had " been now above one whole year stricken with the dart of love "; but he was still rather charmingly and, it seems, genuinely unsure whether he had won her heart. " But if ", he writes,

" it shall please you to do me the office of a true, loyal mistress and friend, and to give yourself up, body and heart, to me who will be and have been your very loyal servitor . . . I promise you not only the name that will be owed to you but also that I will take you for my sole mistress, thrusting all others save you from thought or affection, and to serve you alone."[31] It must have been for Anne, and at about the same time, that Henry wrote the poem comparing his passion to the evergreen holly and saying,

> Now unto my lady
> Promise to her I make
> From all other only
> To her I me betake.

A year later the king is surer of his mistress but clearly impatient of the obstacles that still delay their union. " I trust shortly that our meetings shall not depend upon other men's light handlings but upon your own."[32] Yet he is still the sighing lover as well as the imperious sovereign, for he can write, " Mine own sweetheart, this shall be to advertise you of the great elengeness [loneliness] that I find here since your departing . . . I think your kindness and my fervencies of love causeth it; for otherwise I would not have thought it possible that for so little a while it should have grieved me. . . . Wishing myself (especially [of] an evening) in my sweetheart's arms, whose pretty dukkys [breasts] I trust shortly to kiss."[33]

This young woman who changed so much history has proved singularly elusive to historians. We know little about her and cannot begin to explain her charm. The Venetians, usually rather flattering about the beauties of the English court, thought Anne "not one of the handsomest women in the world". She had a " swarthy complexion, long neck, wide mouth, bosom not much raised, and in fact has nothing but the king's great appetite, and her eyes, which are black and beautiful and take great effect ". Her glory may possibly have been her hair, which was black

and worn loose. She is said to have " sat in it " on her way
to be crowned.[34]

The king may not have been her only lover. Traditionally
the poet Wyatt had pursued her vainly and had been given
cause to complain

> Who list her hunt (I put him out of doubt)
> As well as I may spend his time in vain.
> And graven with diamonds in letters plain
> There is written her fair neck round about :
> 'Noli me tangere, for Caesar's I am,
> And wild for to hold, though I seem tame.'

Henry, too, found her not easily tamed, for it is clear that
she had the strength of will to withhold her favours until
she was sure of being made his queen. It is true that the
final stages of Catherine's divorce had to be hurried because
Anne was already pregnant; but by then the king had gone
too far with his divorce proceedings to draw back; and in
any case he was not going to throw away the chance of a
legitimate male heir.

Henry's passion was genuine enough but it was strangely
mixed with political calculation and with the qualms of a
tormented, if elastic, conscience. Doubts as to the legitimacy
of his marriage with Catherine had been expressed in good
faith and by responsible persons, including her own confessor and Archbishop Warham, before Anne Boleyn was
born. The long succession of miscarriages and still-births
that dogged the first five years of his marriage had already
put the idea of annulment into Henry's mind by 1514—
when English relations with Spain happened to be very
bad.[35] The birth and survival of the Princess Mary (1516)
gave him renewed hope of a male heir. But only miscarriages had followed and by 1525 Catherine was beyond
the age of child-bearing. It was widely held that a woman
could not succeed to the English throne; for Matilda had
not been crowned and the obvious claims of Henry VII's
mother and also of his wife had been tacitly set aside. And,

even if it was legal, the succession of a female raised very plain political problems. Unmarried, she provided no successor. Married to a foreigner, she jeopardised national independence. Married to one of her own subjects, she invited faction fights. In desperation Henry, before he fell in love with Anne, had begun to shower titles on his bastard son,* with a view to making him his heir. It was even proposed that the Pope should be asked to license a marriage between the bastard and his legitimate half-sister Mary. The execution of Buckingham in 1521 was almost solely due to Henry's nervousness about the succession, since he feared that the country might choose its senior noble, rather than a girl, as sovereign.

In the sixteenth century the hand of God was seen in all events. Some, including the queen herself, had wondered whether her still-born children were " a judgment of God, for that her former marriage was made in blood ". Her father (Ferdinand of Aragon) had only consented to it in return for the execution of the innocent Earl of Warwick (surviving nephew of Edward IV) who had seemed a potential rival for the English crown. We need not wonder that Henry himself should have formed the conviction that his queen's failure to provide a man-child was a punishment incurred by his marriage to a deceased brother's wife. Did not the Book of Leviticus say " if a man shall take his brother's wife, it is an unclean thing; . . . they shall be childless " ? There is considerable evidence that Henry's conscience was genuinely troubled and that his dishonesty cannot be thought conscious, if dishonesty it was. We may still doubt whether his conscience would have given quite the prickings and promptings that it did, had he never met with Anne Boleyn. It may be true that " the marriage with his brother's wife " had " crept too near his conscience ",

* This was Henry Fitzroy, Duke of Richmond, son of Elizabeth Blount. Born 1519, died 1536. It was rumoured that he had been poisoned by Anne Boleyn.

as the Lord Chamberlain says in Shakespeare's play; but it was also true, as Suffolk replies, that his conscience had "crept too near another lady".

Nevertheless Henry's concern to have a male heir of indisputable legitimacy cannot be doubted, nor his concern over the possible significance of his wife's miscarriages. Such concerns emerged again years later at the fall of Anne Boleyn. Henry married Jane Seymour with flagrantly indecent haste and he got Cranmer to declare that his marriage with Anne had never been legitimate—on the grounds that he had married the sister of a former mistress. It was doubtful whether this constituted marrying within "prohibited degrees"; nor was it a point which had bothered Cranmer previously; and, since Anne and Catherine were both dead, no one could doubt the legality of the Seymour marriage. But Henry may have wanted to secure Jane's son against any possible rivalry from either of his elder sisters—by bastardising both alike. He may also have realised that Anne Boleyn had always been unpopular. Above all, his conscience may again have been genuinely troubled, since Anne herself had begun to have miscarriages before she fell. In any case, Henry was by that time once again in love, strange as it may seem in view of Jane's undoubted primness. And once his passions were engaged Henry's conscience was apt to become more sensitive as well as more malleable than the consciences of less complicated men.

The annulment of royal marriages which had grown inconvenient was not at all unusual at the time. Henry's amorous sister, Margaret Queen of Scotland, had her second marriage (with the Earl of Angus) dissolved in 1527 on grounds so flimsy that Henry himself sent her a highly moral lecture beseeching her, with what now seems a curious irony, not to bastardise her daughter.[36]* The main obstacle in Henry's own case was the influence of Cather-

* The daughter in question was to become the mother of Darnley.

ine's nephew Charles V over the Pope, who had been the Emperor's prisoner since the sack of Rome in 1527. But for this situation, money and diplomacy would certainly have set the appropriate papal machinery in motion. After all, Henry had been the Pope's most consistent ally among the European sovereigns. The divorce proceedings lasted so long just because Henry felt that it was only a question of time before the Pope would come to his senses; and much of Henry's anger was due to finding that his confidence in Pope Clement had been so misplaced.

One other obstacle there was—the popularity of Catherine with the English people. Indeed, the breach with Rome was relatively popular, or at least acceptable, in England, whereas the divorce itself was not. This is additional evidence that the divorce was the occasion rather than the cause of the English Reformation.

The consequences, momentous though they are, can only be outlined very briefly. They involved not only the severance of England from Catholic Christendom, but a wholesale reconstruction of English society. This left no institution untouched or unchanged. The Crown became sovereign in quite a new sense and might well have become absolute had it not proved necessary to make so much use of parliament and, thereby, to give parliament new powers, new experience, new confidence and new prestige. The work of redistributing monastery land was used by Thomas Cromwell as a means for creating a really professional bureaucratic machine. Government henceforward was no longer to mean the managing of a feudal monarch's personal household and estates, but an impersonal administrative institution which would carry on its work even when the monarch was personally ineffective. Nothing else could have ensured that there was no administrative breakdown, that the king's government was actually carried on, during the disturbed times of Edward VI and Mary.[37]

Henry's government had become revolutionary but there

was no marked revolution in his character and habits as a ruler. No minister was to hold as many titles and offices as Wolsey; and no minister was to have, as Wolsey had had, the king's sole confidence. But Henry had not become more energetic; and Cromwell did quite as much governing as Wolsey, if not more, and played almost as big a part in the direction of policy. The religious, political and social revolutions were no less due to Cromwell than was the revolution in the civil service.

This was important, for it enabled the king to remain relatively popular. He could shelter behind Cromwell or Cranmer, as he sheltered at times behind parliament. He could, if necessary, regain lost popularity by throwing a minister to the wolves, as he did eventually with Cromwell. He may well have remembered how he had first won his people's love by the sacrifice of Empson and Dudley. But, however much he left to his ministers, he left men in no doubt that ministers ruled solely in virtue of the king's favour and by no right of their own. He asserted also, against the rebels in the Pilgrimage of Grace, the king's absolute right to employ any ministers he chose, however low their origins; for the rebels had complained against the " villein blood " in the King's Council and argued that Henry should consult only with his " natural counsellors " the feudal nobility.

Perhaps Cromwell knew the king's caprices and divined therefore that his own term of office was liable to end abruptly. Whatever the reason, Cromwell worked astonishingly fast, and in ten years he changed the face of England. There was, for one thing, a literal physical change in the English landscape—the " bare ruined choirs ". The empty abbeys were seldom left for wind and weather to destroy. They were pulled to pieces by neighbouring squires or townsmen unwilling to let good building materials go a-begging. By Elizabeth's reign, if we may believe a contemporary ballad, the great shrine of Walsingham had fallen low enough.

Level, level with the ground
  The towers do lie,
Which with their golden glittering tops
  Pierced once to the sky!
Where were gates, no gates are now;
  The ways unknown
Where the press of peers did pass,
  While her fame far was blown.
Owls do shriek where the sweetest hymns
  Lately were sung;
Toads and serpents hold their dens
  Where the palmers did throng.[38]

The abbey lands, for the most part, slipped quickly through
the king's fingers and passed on at cheap prices to reward
a whole mass of his servants and supporters, thereby creating
a buyers' market in land.* The boom that followed changed
the social structure of England. In a sense, almost everyone
moved up a step, for even the few surviving bondmen
got their freedom. But some men were able to move up
many steps, since there were fortunes to be made by specu-
lating in real property, by cornering wheat, by enclosing
for sheep-walk and, perhaps most of all, by rack-renting.
Many were hard-faced business men unhampered by
religious scruples, by social conscience or by any old-world
feudal sense of responsibility. Yet the harm done has been
too often exaggerated by taking extreme or untypical examples : and sometimes the " new men " did actual good.
Enclosure, for instance, by no means necessarily involved
suffering; it often brought new affluence to a neighbour-
hood and certainly profited the national economy as a
whole. In any case, the sons and grandsons of the specu-
lators were apt to grow roots of their own and to develop
a new sense of responsibility. They became, in fact, country
gentlemen. Indeed the dissolution of the monasteries made
room in England for the coming of the squires.

* Among the relatively small number of monastic lands retained
by the king were what are now the chief London parks.

For some time, inevitably, the new men were unpopular with the poor, and were not altogether trusted in government circles. Pamphleteers, preachers and statesmen all complained that too many of the gentry were idle, boorish, self-seeking, irresponsible. Burghley made plans to have more of them sent to the universities; and Spenser hoped that *The Faerie Queene* might soften their manners and teach them chivalry and public spirit. The statesman and the poet were both aware that the new ruling class needed educating up to its task. In the end the gentry absorbed their lessons. Before Elizabeth died they had founded or refounded the oldest grammar schools of England. They had worked assiduously on the Justice's bench. They had been outspoken in the House of Commons. They had written some great poetry. They had learnt to " haul and draw with the mariners ", as Drake had bidden them. They had even taxed themselves to keep the unemployed from starving. A number of them had developed a high seriousness which took them into the Puritan camp. They had already become the most public-spirited, the most courageous, the most resourceful, the most energetic, the most broadly-based ruling class that the world had seen since Periclean Athens. Nor did they much abuse the liberty which they were to win from the Stuart kings, nor keep it wholly to themselves. On the one hand they seldom lost the common touch, and on the other they were not uncultivated. They would know the price of oats or pigs; they would ride hard, swear hard, drink hard. But they would also quote from Ovid or from Horace and build many of the most beautiful houses in the world. They established a social tradition of marvellous solidity and yet produced the long and brilliant line of English eccentrics. It is sometimes overlooked by sentimentalists that the Catholic Middle Ages also had a ruling class and that it was not wholly public-spirited.

By establishing the new men, Henry in effect prevented himself from establishing a despotism. He knew that when his aims clashed seriously with the interests of the gentry it was he who would have to give way, as he did over the Statute of Wills and Uses which was thought damaging to land-owners. He knew that he must keep out of war because the gentry would not pay the taxes war would involve and because the merchants would not tolerate interruption of the cloth trade with Flanders. He knew that the lawyers would not accept any substitution of the Roman for the Common Law. He knew that Parliament had to be left free to amend or even to reject government bills. Even when Parliament (in 1539) recognised what was already constitutional fact, namely, that royal proclamations had the full force of law, the act was so worded as to imply that parliamentary statutes were the *best* kind of law. The statute has sometimes been called the high-water mark of Tudor despotism, but was in fact nothing of the sort.

By establishing the new men, Henry had also done something else. He had given them, in their abbey lands, a vested interest in the continuance of the breach with Rome. It soon emerged, too, that neither he nor the new men could afford half-measures, that it was not possible for England to remain anti-papal and yet in some sense Catholic. The king could not afford to leave men in any doubt as to the absolute legitimacy of his second and third marriages. Nor could they be allowed to think, as More did, that in some fields there was a higher law than the king's. By the same token, the gentry could not leave room for questioning the validity of their title-deeds. In time, some of them acquired an appetite for further ecclesiastical properties and supported a movement to abolish episcopacy, in the hope that laymen might enjoy episcopal as well as monastic endowments.

But the king and the gentry were not the whole of England. Although many quite small men acquired, indirectly, some stake in monastic property, the common people as a whole had not been gainers. They escaped very little even of ecclesiastical taxation, which continued to be levied, although it now went into royal or secular coffers. The people suffered also some social loss, though it has sometimes been assessed too highly. They had fewer hospitals and, for a time, fewer schools and less accommodation for benighted travellers. Nor did the people like the new rack-renting landlords. No one, rich or poor, understood the reasons for the rapid price-rise of this period; and therefore the poor were apt to blame the rich unjustly for hardships which were really due to newly-found sources of gold and silver and, above all, to the government's debasement of the coin.

Naturally the people could understand no better the constitutional subtleties of the royal supremacy. No less naturally their religious sentiments were, for the most part, conservative and Catholic. Many were shocked at the image-breaking of Thomas Cromwell's commissioners. Agrarian and religious grievances were inextricably entangled in the causes of the Pilgrimage of Grace. Yet, in the end, it may have been the people who, unwittingly, forced the king to approach more nearly to doctrinal Protestantism.

The people had been taught for centuries that it was the Pope alone, with his keys, who could unlock for them the gates of Heaven. They were worried now about their prospects of salvation. Great as the king was, could he save their souls and, if not, where were they to look? By 1536 Cranmer was already reporting to Henry that he had been forced to tell the people that the canon laws which were now enforced by royal authority had not been retained because they " remit sin ". Sins, he had said, were remitted solely " by the death of our Saviour Christ Jesus. . . . It was too much injury to Christ to impute the remission of our sins to any laws or ceremonies of man's making.[39]" In other words, Cranmer had been compelled, perhaps not unwillingly, to preach Protestant theology. He had had to tell the people that they must save their own souls by having faith in the Merits of Christ, that no other man and no human institution could procure salvation for them.

In any case, Henry had given the English Bible to the people. The long-term consequences for English religion and for English literature are beyond calculation. We do not know the king's motives. He may have been influenced by Cromwell, or by Cranmer, or by Anne Boleyn. He may have hoped that an authorised version would undo the harm done by the numerous clandestine copies of Tyndale's version which were already circulating. He may have believed for a time that his own bishops were more serious than in fact they were over the project of producing a version of their own. But, in the end, it was Coverdale's and Rogers' versions that were given to the people and indeed thrust under their noses, since the Bible was compulsorily displayed in every church. Within a generation Bible-reading, though it had not made a Protestant majority, had made far more Protestants than any government could possibly have rooted out. Perhaps Henry knew that the revolution was already out of his control and that he had better give it his blessing with as good a grace as he could muster. At the end Henry must have accepted the necessity for the revolution to go further still, since he bequeathed to his son a Council dominated by radical reformers.

Henry's development from gaiety to grimness, from the liberal humanist to the masterful tyrant, was due in part to his unmitigated selfishness, to his determination to have his own way whatever the cost. There was substance in Sir Robert Naunton's later verdict that Henry had never spared a man in his anger nor a woman in his lust. But the change was also due to a sense of frustration. He had counted unavailingly on the Pope's giving way, on a secure succession to the throne, on national unity. There is something pathetic in his last speech to Parliament (in 1545) and there is no need to think it insincere. It was a plea for charity between Englishmen. " Charity and concord is not amongst you but discord and dissension beareth rule in every place. . . . I am very sorry to know and to hear how unreverently that most precious jewel, the Word of God, is disputed, rhymed, sung, and jangled in every ale-house and tavern. . . . And yet I am even as much sorry that the readers of the same follow it in doing, so faintly and so coldly.[40]"

For years Henry had been ill and in pain. Even as a young man he had suffered from headaches. Now he was corpulent and dropsical, with an appalling ulcer or fistula in his leg which rendered him at times speechless and black in the face with pain. He may, in his later years, have suffered from some glandular maladjustment. He grew enormous, needing a " device " to carry him upstairs, and could scarcely get through an ordinary doorway. In his last portrait engraved by Cornelis Matsys, the king's eyes have become slits peering between bloated lids. According to Fuller, " he had a body and a half, very abdominous and unwieldy with fat. And it was death to him to be dieted, so great his appetite, and death to him not to be dieted, so great his corpulency." In his last illness " flame met with fire, the anguish of the sore with an hot and impatient temper ", so that no one dared approach him, still less tell him that he was dying.[41]

He had always been self-indulgent and self-willed, but a combination of illness and misfortune rendered him almost megalomaniac. He had to impose his personality upon everyone and everything. A straw which may show the direction of the wind can be found in the coinage of the realm. For two centuries the head of Edward I had done duty for the sovereign's image. Henry VII broke with the past by putting his own portrait on the coins, but for sixteen years his son left this unchanged. On the eve of the Reformation a new coinage was struck, bearing the new Caesar's image and superscription. Henceforward the common man was not to buy a loaf of bread without fingering his master's picture.

Illness and frustration made Henry strike out in all directions, kicking against the pricks. Two wives paid with their heads for what may well have been unfaithfulness, and must at least have been serious indiscretions. Jane Seymour, perhaps the most loved of his wives, died in childbed; and it was obvious that his only male heir would succeed to the throne as a child. Henry was not going to let his heir have any rivals for the throne. He struck at every surviving Plantagenet on whom he could lay his hands— Courtenay and the Poles, including the aged and harmless Countess of Salisbury who was beheaded in circumstances of quite peculiar horror and indignity : and on his death-bed Henry almost brought down the Howards, the greatest noble family in England. Surrey the poet had asked for trouble by quartering the royal arms with his own and by having been talked of as a potential husband for the Princess Mary. His father Norfolk, who was to have gone to execution the day after Henry died, had long been the leader of the counter-revolutionaries; and he had perhaps been spared so long, only because of his popularity and social and military prestige. Henry had said years before that there was no head in his kingdom so noble " but he would make it fly " if his will was crossed.

It was not only the great who suffered. When in 1544 the king learnt that he had been deserted by his supposed friends in Scotland he wrote in terrible and ringing prose to Hertford, who commanded the invading English army, telling him to " sack Leith and burn and subvert it and all the rest, putting man woman and child to fire and sword without exception . . . and extend the like extremities and destructions in all towns and villages whereunto ye may reach conveniently, not forgetting among all the rest so to spoil and turn upside down the Cardinal's town of St Andrews, as the upper stone may be the nether, and not one stick stand by another, sparing no creature alive within the same. . . . Furthermore . . . you shall take order with the Wardens that the borderers in Scotland may be still tormented and occupied as much as can be conveniently, now specially that it is seed-time, from the which if they may be kept and not suffered to sow their grounds, they shall by the next year be brought to such a penury as they shall not be able to live nor abide the country."[42] The kindly Hertford wrote that he " could not sleep this night for thinking of the king's determination for Leith ".[43]

Nor was Henry more merciful to the disaffected among his own subjects. When the king was told of the Lincolnshire rising in 1541 he said that he had " an evil people to govern " and that he would make them so poor that they would have no more power to rebel. By his taxation and by the debasement of the coins he nearly succeeded. And yet he never lost his popularity with the great majority of his subjects and never found any lack of willing hands to combat rebels or repel threats of invasion. The people, including women and children, would take to digging trenches or planting palisades before the government gave orders.[44]

Most extraordinary of all are the self-incriminations, on the scaffold, of Henry's victims. A few protested moral innocence, but none claimed that their sentence was illegal. Buckingham, in Shakespeare's play, avows that

To the law I bear no malice for my death,
It has done upon the premises but justice . . .
. . . I had my trial,
And, must needs say, a noble one.

He had his counterparts in Anne Boleyn's brother, Lord Rochford, who said he " had not come there to preach, but to serve as mirror and example ", or in Cromwell himself when he said, " I am by the law condemned to die . . . I have offended my prince, for the which I ask him heartily forgiveness."

In our own day we have heard not dissimilar confessions from the victims of totalitarian governments. But Henry's victims had not been " brain-washed " and had not been pre-conditioned by a party discipline. It is possible of course that they had been threatened with torture or with the full penalty for treason, namely disembowelling, unless they made appropriate confessions. Tyndale once hinted at

something of the sort. " When any great man is put to
death, how his confessor intreateth him, and what penance
is enjoined him, concerning what he shall say when he
cometh unto the place of execution, I could guess at a
practice that might make men's ears glow."[45] Yet it is at
least equally possible that the victims genuinely felt bound
to uphold the principle of authority even with their dying
breaths. Much of that psychological discipline was Henry's
doing. He had not wholly failed, for he had contrived to
create in the minds of his subjects a new conception of the
state and to touch their imaginations in a way that no
English king had done before. He had embodied and
personified in their eyes that self-contained, self-sufficing,
sovereign *imperium* for the sake of which he had shed
innocent blood, broken the clergy, shattered the unity of
Christendom and defied with impunity all the powers of
Europe.

Napoleon is reported to have said that the use of blank
cartridge against the mob instead of his " whiff of grape-
shot " would have involved a cruel waste of life. Something
of the sort might be said of Henry's ruthlessness. Religious
and social revolution was almost bound to overtake the
England which he inherited. Henry saw to it that the revolution was got under government control. By doing so he
minimised the inevitable civil strife and bloodshed. And he
contrived that the revolution should make and not unmake
his sovereign state. He caused it also to be a revolution by
due process of law and a revolution in which parliament and
people were, at least technically, his accomplices. By doing
so he filled men with a revolutionary or crusading ardour,
not so much for the new religion as for the new realm
which Henry was the first to call an Empire.

CHAPTER V

EDWARD THE SIXTH

1547-1553

Historians have been apt to dismiss the reigns of Edward and of Mary as an almost irrelevant interlude in the development of Tudor England, as a backwater remote from the main stream, or as a trough between two waves. At best the period has been seen as no more than a salutary object lesson demonstrating to Englishmen the dangers of extreme courses, thereby inculcating the lesson England had to learn before settling down to the Elizabethan "middle way". Yet it is scarcely adequate to put into a parenthesis the years which first rooted the Protestant religion permanently in English soil and later sent the exiles to bring back the Puritan religion from abroad. The same years restored to the clergy, to the great advantage of the nation, their apostolic married state.* The same years confirmed the English in their hatred of foreign interference and seared England for ever with the Fires of Smithfield. They were the years, too, which tested the constitutional engine constructed by Henry VIII and Thomas Cromwell, and proved that it could survive reckless driving and could even survive being put into reverse. The England of these years was also the England which first heard the cadences of Cranmer's Prayer Book and the unmuffled voice of Latimer.

It was an England which experienced under Somerset the

* It is worth a moment's reflection to recall how many great Englishmen and Englishwomen, from Nelson and Montgomery to Jane Austen and the Brontës, were born in clerical families. Nor must we forget that the more highly we think of mediaeval monks, the more highly (from a eugenic point of view) we must regret their sterilisation.

first government to attempt social justice and also, under Dudley, the first government to allow quite naked exploitation by the *nouveaux riches*. It was too an England which, thanks to the genius of Gresham, survived what was probably the worst financial crisis of her history. And, if it was the England which lost Calais, it was also the England which came very near to conquering the Scots and sent her first argosies upon the open seas. Before Mary died English voyagers had been to Mexico and Guinea, to Nova Zembla and Cape Breton; and one traveller, Jenkinson, had reached Bokhara.

At Edward's accession an intelligent observer might well have asked certain questions. Could Henry rule from the tomb? How much of Henry's system had depended on his own personality? Could a Council, trained for so long to carry out one man's private will, now develop a mind and policy of its own? Could the Council have its own policy and yet remain public-spirited? Would it become a self-seeking " gang " or break up into factions? Could the Wars of the Roses return? Would the country accept things done by others in the king's name? Above all, could the social and religious revolution stand still? Was it inevitable that there should be either conservative reaction or else further moves in a revolutionary direction? This last point Henry himself had decided. He had preferred to let the revolution proceed rather than have his work undone. He had ensured that the Councillors should be drawn from the new men; but it was soon clear that he had failed in his other object, that of putting the Crown into commission. The Council had become so accustomed to one man's rule that it rapidly acquiesced in the virtual *coup d'état* which made Somerset, the king's eldest uncle, Lord Protector. It remained to be seen whether a regent could deal successfully with his rivals or resist the temptation to usurp the throne. Somerset was to fail against his rivals, and his successor, Dudley, was to succumb to the temptation.

Nevertheless, distressing though the history of the reign

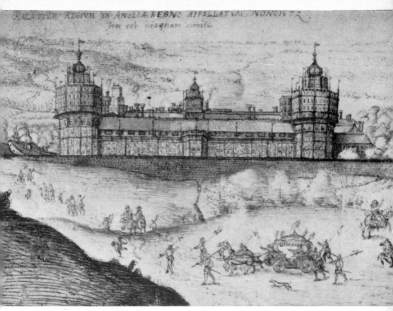

REGIVM IN ANGLIÆ REGNO APPELLATVR NONCIVTZ
Hoc est usquam simile

"THE CLOUD-CAPP'D TOWERS": NONESUCH PALACE IN 1568
from a drawing by Joris Hofnaegal

"THE GORGEOUS PALACES": HAMPTON COURT IN 1558
from a drawing by Antonius Wynegaard

Anno ɧ o ɜ ʒe octobꝛ ꝛmaꥱo ꝫenꝛicꝫ vıɪ bancıꝛꝫ ꝛege illꝰꝼtꝛꝰıꝼꝼıᵐ
oꝛdınata ꝑ ꝫeꝛmãı ʒınck ꝼo ꝛeꝷıe .... ꝫılꝼen ...

HENRY VII HOLDING A TUDOR ROSE

by a Flemish artist, possibly Michiel Sitium; dated 1505

HENRY VII: *terracotta bust by Pietro Torrigiano*

HENRY VII. PROBABLY THE MOST AUTHENTIC LIKENESS
from the funeral effigy in Westminster Abbey

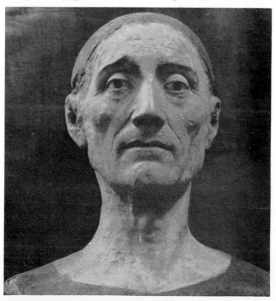

HENRY VIII AS A CHILD
by an unknown French artist

KING SOLOMON. BELIEVED BY THE
WRITER TO BE A PORTRAIT OF HENRY VIII
from a window in King's College Chapel, Cambridge

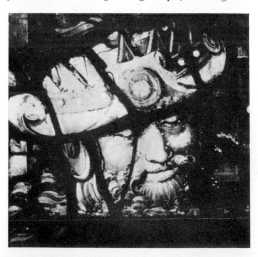

HENRY VIII AGED 25.
THE EARLIEST KNOWN PORTRAIT OF HENRY AS KING
by Jean Perreal, Franco-Flemish painter, 1516

CATHERINE
OF ARAGON

*by an unknown artist,
after Johannes Corvus*

ANN BOLEYN.
PROBABLY THE BEST
EXISTING LIKENESS

by Hans Holbein

HENRY VIII IN
MIDDLE LIFE
from a medal

HENRY VIII IN OLD AGE
engraving by Cornelis Matsys, 1544

EDWARD VI

*reproduced, from the portrait after Hans Holbein,
by Gracious Permission of H.M. The Queen*

MARY I
by Hans Eworth, 1554

THE PRINCESS ELIZABETH, AGED ABOUT 13

*by an unknown artist; reproduced
by Gracious Permission of H.M. The Queen*

MARY I

*from a medal, by
Jacopo da Trezzo,
struck to commemorate
her marriage to
Philip of Spain, 1555*

ELIZABETH I

miniature by Nicholas Hilliard

ELIZABETH WITH TIME AND DEATH

from the painting attributed to Marc Gheerarts the Elder;
at Corsham Court, Wiltshire

was to be, there was no return to feudal anarchy. There was gross rapacity and shameless caballing but there was no serious civil war until Mary was actually proclaimed queen. There were sporadic rebellions, but they were less dangerous than the risings against Henry, and they were all put down. The machinery of government was monstrously misused but it did not come to a standstill. England was to have a corrupt and an unjust government but not an ineffective government.

There was a seemingly untroubled point of rest in the very centre of the storm. It was the mind of a small orphan boy who was the last Tudor king of England. He came to the throne when he was just over nine and died just before he was sixteen. And yet we know his mind better than that of any other Tudor, for we have his own full journal of his reign. It might be called the first of all English diaries. On certain matters, notably the trial of Somerset, the boy's journal is much the best surviving evidence.

It is arguable that potentially Edward was the ablest of all the Tudors. It is also possible that, had he lived, he would have been the least attractive. As to his precocity we have independent testimony, not only from courtiers and tutors, but from foreign visitors like Cardan, whose charlatanry on the causation of comets the boy nearly exposed during a conversation conducted in highly technical Latin.[1] Edward wrote essays in French on the royal supremacy in the church and on the reform of ecclesiastical abuses. He knew Greek well and read some Aristotle early in his fourteenth year. Besides his journal, which shows an obviously intelligent grasp of diplomatic affairs, he wrote memoranda on harbours and fortifications and on the very complicated question of currency reform. In another memorandum, proposing reforms for the Order of the Garter, he recommends that the order be free from all associations with Saint George because of the popish and superstitious aura surrounding any saint. Edward was an assiduous attender of sermons and took copious notes, sometimes—for practice or amusement—writing English words in Greek letters. He played the lute and liked listening to Sternhold's new metrical psalms.

From a letter written by his tutor Richard Cox, when the boy was not quite eight years old, we learn that the prince had already " expugned and conquered a great number of the captains of ignorance ", could conjugate any Latin verb perfectly, " unless it be anomalum. . . . Hath made already forty or fifty pretty Latin verses. . . . Is now ready to enter into Cato, to some proper and profitable fables of Aesop. . . . Every day readeth a portion of Solomon's Proverbs, wherein he delighteth much; and learneth there . . . to beware of strange and wanton women and . . . to be thankful to him who telleth him of his faults."[2]

Yet in physique this prodigy was not weedy or unattractive. Though a little under-sized for his age and, according to Cardan, slightly short-sighted and with one shoulder higher than the other, he was lively, gracious and good-looking, with fair hair and gray eyes. He had tried to walk before his first birthday, and " when the minstrels played " the infant, we are told, " danced and played so wantonly that he could not stand still ".[3] And, although as a child he had been frightened at the appearance of some unprepossessing German envoys,[4] he was certainly not without spirit. On one occasion a schoolfellow persuaded him to use " thundering oaths " as being appropriate to his royal dignity, for which the king was admonished and his companion whipped.[5] Tudor education contained no injunctions against " sneaking ".

Mingled with affairs of state in Edward's journal are accounts of his sports and pastimes, such as the occasion when he watched " the bear hunted in the river, and also wild-fire cast out of the boats, and many pretty conceits ", or the occasion when his side won at prisoner's base. In April 1550, he writes, " I lost the challenge at shooting at rounds and won at rovers "; and a month later he is dissatisfied with the umpiring in a contest in tilting at the ring.

" My band touched often, which was counted as nothing, and took never, which seemed very strange, and so the prize was of my side lost."[6] If, however, he spent too long at play instead of work, he would reprove himself, saying " We forget ourselves . . . that would not chose *substantia pro accidente*."[7] Nevertheless he enjoyed a sight-seeing progress through the south of England, which included " good hunting and good cheer "; or showing off his riding and archery to the French ambassador. Nor did he, until his final illness (which lasted only seven months), lack robustness. He suffered from a quartan ague at the age of three; and he had something diagnosed as a combination of smallpox and measles in April 1552 but six weeks later was " running at the ring " in Greenwich Park.[8]

Edward could impress visitors with his apparent charm and with his " piety and sweetness of disposition ".[9] But, perhaps in self-protection, he seems to have acquired from very early days a cold, detached reserve. It is almost certain that he was fond of two people only in the course of his life —his favourite tutor Sir John Cheke and his favourite stable companion Barnaby Fitzpatrick, a young Irish noble. Once when Cheke was very ill and expected on all hands to die, the king said, " He will not die at this time, for this morning I begged his life from God in my prayers, and obtained it."[10]

To Barnaby the king wrote his only intimate and informal letters, although a slightly priggish tone occasionally obtrudes. " Shortly ", he wrote when Barnaby was at the French court, " we will prove how ye have profited in the French tongue, for within a while we will write to you in French." He also advised his friend : " For women, as far forth as ye may, avoid their company. Yet if the French King command you, you may sometimes dance, so measure be your mean. Else apply yourself to riding, shooting or tennis, with such honest games. Not forgetting sometime, when you have leisure, your learning, chiefly reading of the Scripture. Thus I write, not doubting but you would have done so had I not written, but to spur you on." Perhaps Barnaby was justified in replying, " Ye make me think the care ye take for me is more fatherly than friendly."[11]

Only on one occasion is Edward reported to have laughed. It was after a service on St George's Day and he asked the Lord Treasurer who St George had been. " If it please your Majesty," he was told, " I did never in any history read of St George, but only in *Legenda Aurea*, where it is thus set down, that St George out with his sword and ran the dragon through with his spear." Whereupon the king, " having some time vented himself with laughing, replied ' I pray you, my Lord, and what did he do with his sword the while?' "[12]

That Edward was priggish, especially over the Protestant religion in which he was brought up, cannot well be doubted, although we need not necessarily believe Fuller's story about the king's refusal to stand on a Bible in order to reach a high shelf.[13] If there is any truth in Sir John Hayward's story that, at his coronation, Edward was presented with three swords representing his three kingdoms but demanded a fourth, the Bible which he called " the Sword of the Spirit . . . to be preferred before these swords ", no doubt the incident was not unrehearsed.[14]

Edward's coldness emerges most clearly in his attitude toward his two Seymour uncles. Undoubtedly his uncle Thomas, the Lord High Admiral, had committed the grossest indiscretions and had most shamelessly intrigued for power. Yet he had, with whatever motives, been kind to the boy, and it was ungenerous of Edward to allow it to be put in evidence at the Admiral's trial that he had secretly augmented the boy king's pocket-money.[15] His elder uncle, the Protector, Edward patently disliked. On his own admission, when the Admiral said to him that Somerset was old and might not live long, Edward had replied, " It were better he should die."[16] And he never forgave Somerset for taking him by night to Windsor, almost by force, in an attempt to retain power. Windsor in any case he hated; for there, he wrote, " Methinks I am in prison. Here be no galleries nor no gardens to walk in."[17] When Somerset was executed the king's entry in his journal is somewhat bleak. It reads : " The Duke of Somerset had his head cut off upon Tower Hill between eight and nine a clock in the morning."

Edward is likely to have had his mind poisoned against Somerset, first perhaps by his younger uncle the Admiral Seymour, and later by John Dudley. The king's version of Somerset's trial is obviously Dudley's version. His preference for Dudley over Somerset would suggest that Edward was a poor judge of men. But we must remember that Somerset had, by virtual self-appointment, made himself the boy's guardian and may have lectured him unpalatably. Furthermore, Somerset was so busy with affairs of state and was for so long away on his Scottish campaign that he lost his chance of acquiring real influence over the boy. It may well be simply that he was not " good with children ", whereas Dudley evidently was. Dudley certainly took more trouble and had greater opportunity. Perhaps he impressed the ardently Protestant young king with his apparently greater zeal for the Protestant cause. At any rate, since the king was by no means the only person who succumbed to his influence, Dudley must have had personality or charm; and it is certain that he was able, energetic and a born intriguer. Nor can we rule out the possibility that Edward was uneasily aware of what had happened to the last boy king of England whose uncle had been Regent.

The result of these personal factors was singularly tragic, for Somerset might have done much for England, whereas Dudley brought her very near to ruin. The history of Edward's reign is inevitably the history of the tensions between these two. Both were personally ambitious and both feathered their own nests rapaciously and shamelessly from the spoils of the Reformation. But Dudley's ambition and rapacity were naked and unalloyed, whereas Somerset combined his with a genuine social conscience and a genuine belief in toleration. He repealed Henry VIII's statute which had made spoken words treason; and during Somerset's rule not a single person was tortured or executed for his or her religious views. Joan Boacher was condemned by Cranmer for heresy but Somerset refused to sign her death warrant, and she was not burnt till six months after his fall. Two recalcitrant bishops, Gardiner and Bonner, were deprived and temporarily imprisoned with very little rigour; and a few Anabaptists were condemned to "bear a faggot" in public penance at Paul's Cross. This must be a record unique for any English government before 1689.

Somerset's social policy was no less humane, whether or not it was practicable or well-advised. Indeed it was largely on account of his humanity that he was overthrown. If it were not known that he was greedy for power and for riches, that he pulled down an aisle of St Paul's and had plans for pulling down Westminster Abbey in order to furnish his own palace, he might well be compared with Shakespeare's Brutus. He certainly intrigued without having any talent for intriguing, and certainly he intrigued partly "in a general honest thought and common good to all". Like Brutus also, he had a mind too academic and aloof and too impervious to facts. He had no sense of political realities or of what was politically possible. He had no gift for keeping in with anyone who mattered. He started too many policies at once and had not the resolution to push any of them through in the teeth of opposition. Whenever he was faced with opposition he handled it too gently.

Yet Somerset was a brave and brilliant soldier, as he proved in his first move after coming to power,—the war with Scotland. The Scots had repudiated their pledge to betroth the infant Mary Stuart to the English king; and Somerset's invasion was a punitive expedition to avenge the breach of promise. In his view it was also a war "to make an end to all wars, to conclude an eternal and perpetual peace". His plans for the new united kingdom were characteristically liberal and would have given the Scots complete home rule and free trade. But Scotland was too proud to accept union at the sword's point, and she had long been virtually a satellite of France. In any case, Somerset's burning of the Border Abbeys, of Leith, of Holyrood and of most of Edinburgh, in the campaigns of 1542 to 1544, had not endeared him to the Scots. At Pinkie Cleugh (September 4th, 1547) he inflicted on them a defeat even more shattering than Flodden. He was considerably outnumbered but made the fullest use of his superior artillery and vastly superior tactics, which included combined operations with an English galley. At least ten Scots fell for every Englishman. But the English army was only provisioned for a month, and Somerset was distracted both by war with France and by his religious and social schemes for England. With a strong Protestant and pro-English faction in Scotland, it was more than possible that Somerset would have conquered the country had he not withdrawn, leaving garrisons in a few well-chosen strongholds and, this time, sparing Edinburgh.

In England, too, Somerset showed himself almost at once as a man of action, capable of rapid decision and not afraid of radical change. The changes that he made were bold enough, but by abjuring Henry VIII's terroristic methods he gravely handicapped his chances of success. There was nothing remarkably unorthodox in Cranmer's *Book of Homilies* or in the new ecclesiastical Injunctions of 1547, except that the Litany and the lessons had to be read in English and that processions and images were now frowned upon. Yet it was clear that the government was no longer censoring the Protestant preachers; and conservatives like Gardiner took immediate alarm. The clergy, however, made no protest when parliament repealed all Henry VIII's anti-heresy laws. Convocation indeed petitioned for the abolition of clerical celibacy. Curiously enough the opposition to clerical marriage came from lay magnates. Not long before, the Duke of Norfolk had expressed their inner thoughts when he said that he feared lest the clergy " will perchance marry with our and other gentlemen's daughters and so have their dowries, jointures and lands with them; and at last ye shall see the Bishops have all our lands too."[18]

There was substance in the view taken by the contemporary French traveller Étienne Perlin that the English were given " only to vanity and ambition and merchandise "; and undoubtedly the Spanish ambassador shrewdly anatomised the spirit of the times when he noted that a commission had been set up to enquire into the clergy's " knowledge, manner of life and income. . . . It may well turn out that the question of income is the principal one."[19] It was so indeed. The new Protestant bishops had to accept vastly diminished stipends. Ponet, on succeeding Gardiner at Winchester, had to surrender to the Crown all the lands attached to the see (worth some £3000 a year) and receive in exchange other lands bringing him 2000 marks (circa £1330).[20] Coverdale at Exeter had to accept an income of £500 which was only one-third of his predecessor's.[21] Hooper was made to hold the sees of Worcester and Gloucester in plurality so that the income of the see of Gloucester (newly made by Henry VIII) might revert to the Crown.[22] Before the end of Edward's reign the whole of the church plate had been requisitioned, leaving nothing but one chalice to each parish church; while in Devonshire, after the rebellion there, even the church bells were melted down, saving only " the least of the ring ".[23]

Somerset was personally greedy and strongly anti-clerical but his policy was far from anti-social. Indeed it is likely that he thought his anti-clericalism to be furthering the social good. He certainly tried hard to put a stop to the depredations of the rich. Latimer his *protégé*, denounced their greed with courage, with passion and with a voice of thunder. Hales, Somerset's right-hand man, took active steps to fix rents, to pull down enclosures and to plough up pasture land for tillage. The policy was by no means revolutionary; it involved no new legislation, merely the proper enforcement of existing laws. But it was not worldly-wise. Paradoxically yet perhaps inevitably it provoked rebellion, for the oppressed will revolt more often through hope than through despair. But revolutionary activity, when a liberal government has attained power, can play into the hands of brutal and unscrupulous reactionaries. It can provide them with the excuses they require; and it should be known for what it is, the most criminal of political follies.

Somerset, for all his military prowess, was too generous and too liberal to take severe or effective action against rebels with whom he was at least half in sympathy. His half-heartedness gave his enemies a pretext for overthrowing him on trumped-up charges of conspiring against the lives of his fellow Councillors. His religious policy had lost him the support of the conservatives and his social policy that of the newly rich. A scapegoat was needed for military and diplomatic defeats at the hands of France, for the appalling state of the finances, and for the disorders in the countryside. His fellow Councillors were either actively behind his rival Dudley or, like Cranmer and Cecil, anxious not to back a losing horse. Like the Lord Treasurer (Paulet, Marquess of Winchester) most of them preferred to sway with the willow rather than to stand with the oak.

One of them, Paget, had been too close a friend of the Protector to escape temporary disgrace—on the ostensible grounds that he held dignities too high for one who " was no gentleman of blood ".[24] But Paget was so able and so wily that his fortunes soon revived. Besides, he could if necessary have shown proof that he had warned Somerset months earlier against the policy he had been pursuing. Paget's letter, which might have been addressed by Cassius to Brutus, is highly revealing of the attitude which enabled a Tudor statesman to survive and also of the political temper of the times.

Paget cannot resist the maddening " I told you so ". " I told your Grace the truth and was not believed : well, now your Grace seeth it. . . . And what is the cause? Your own lenity, your softness, your opinion to be good to the poor;

the opinion of such as saith to your Grace, ' Oh ! sir, there
was never man had the hearts of the poor as you have !
Oh ! the commons pray for you, sir, they say, " God save
your life ".' " Paget knows, he says, that the Protector has
meant well, although a hint is dropped that others suspect
him of sinister intentions. But it is meaning well that has
done all the harm. " It is great pity, as the common pro-
verb goeth, . . . that ever warm weather should do harm.
It is pity that your too much gentleness should be an
occasion of so great an evil as is now chanced in England
by these rebels." Society is held together by brittle bonds;
it " doth consist and is maintained by means of religion and
laws. And these two or one wanting, farewell all just
society, farewell kings, government, justice, all other virtue.
And in cometh commonalty, sensuality, iniquity, and all
kinds of vice and mischief." But Somerset has failed to
produce a settled religion. " The use of the old religion is
forbidden . . . and the use of the new is not yet printed ",
or at least not " printed in the stomachs " of the people,
" what countenance soever men make outwardly to please
them in whom they see the power resteth." Above all,
Somerset has not enforced the law; and consequently " the
foot taketh upon him the part of the head, and Commons
is become a king; a king appointing conditions and laws to
the governors, saying, ' Grant this and that, and we will go
home.' " It might be Menenius Agrippa speaking. The
bottom has fallen out of that ordered universe which so
mesmerised the Tudor mind.

The Protector, Paget argues, should have been cruel first
and kind afterwards; he should " at the first stir " have
" caused justice to have been done in solemn fashion to the
terror of others, and then to have granted pardons ". As it
is, Somerset's clemency has acted like a papal pardon
" which rather, upon hope of a pardon, gave men occasion
and courage to sin, than to amend their faults ". The poor
have been encouraged to air every grievance and to expect,
as a right, to have it remedied. It is also suggested that their

grievances are no worse than those of the poor in other countries, nor than their own during the preceding fifty years. Henry VIII, already a name to conjure with, kept all his subjects, we are told, "in due obedience" and did so by the ruthless "maintenance of justice in due course". Weakness and temporising can only lead to greater bloodshed in the long run, as it did, says Paget, in the German peasants' revolt. The only remedy now is to hang at least six of the ring-leaders in every disaffected shire and to imprison or conscript into the army a good many more. "Give them no good words, or make no promise in nowise."

"Your Grace may say", Paget writes, "I shall lose the hearts of the people : of the good people you shall not, and of the evil it maketh no matter. By this means you shall be dread, which hitherto you are not. . . . By this means you shall deliver the King an obedient realm." Blood and iron are required and no more talk of "Liberty, Liberty". "And put no more so many irons in the fire at once, as you have done this twelve-month. War with Scotland, with France; . . . commissions out for this matter : new laws for this : proclamations for another : one in another's neck so thick that they be not set by among the people."[25]

Paget claimed to have his feet on the ground. "Alas," he wrote to Sir William Petre, "we must not think that heaven is here but that we live in a world." Yet it is arguable that Somerset was not bound to fail. There are "soft" facts as well as hard facts, and a statesman can be powerful if he embodies the aspirations and ideals of humble people. It is as real a fact as any other that men hold ideals, and we have no right to assume that the man whose power rests upon them is foredoomed. Woodrow Wilson happened to be outmanoeuvred but Lincoln and Roosevelt were not; still less Mahatma Gandhi.

The fall of Somerset is sinister. He was accused of conspiring against his fellow Councillors' lives, but some of the evidence was obtained by torture, and some depended on the word of alleged accomplices who were pardoned with suspicious alacrity and were soon high in Dudley's favour. The charges that have real significance are those in which Somerset was accused of declaring that the nobles and the gentry had caused "the dearth of things, whereby the people rose and did reform things themselves"; or of causing "many and sundry commissions to be made out concerning enclosures"; of comforting and encouraging rebellion; of saying that "since Parliament was loth" to make reforms, the people "had good cause" to take the law into their own hands.[26]

The king himself reports in his journal that Somerset had threatened "if he were overthrown, he would run through London and cry 'Liberty! Liberty!' to raise the apprentices and rabble". Somerset denied this, but such a plan, had it been tried, might well have succeeded. When it was falsely rumoured that the Protector had been acquitted, the crowd round Westminster Hall "made such a shriek and casting up of caps that it was heard into the Long Acre beyond Charing Cross" and the Duke was escorted to the Tower with "the people crying 'God save him!' all the way as he went".[27] The same false rumour caused the bells to ring and bonfires to be lighted as far away as Bath; and for long afterwards the name of "the Good Duke" was held in affection up and down the country. At his execution many dipped their handkerchiefs in his blood, supposing it to have the virtue of a martyr's. When Mary came to the throne she found it advisable to recall, in her very first Act of Parliament, that "honourable and noble persons" had "of late . . . suffered shameful death not accustomed to nobles".

Somerset failed to save England for the poor or to halt the social revolution that was to make England a nation of shop-keepers and of squires. Yet he has left his mark on English life, for it was his government which set in motion those processes that were to make the English religion a Protestant religion and the English Church an "Anglican" Church.

Yet Somerset's religious measures were moderate in most respects. Several of them emanated from the bishops, very few of whom could be called definitely Protestant. It was Convocation which allowed clerical marriage and restored to the laity Communion in both kinds, thus reverting to the obvious intention of the Founder of Christianity. There was some official deprecation of saints' day customs that were deemed " idolatrous ", but prayers for the dead and auricular confession were expressly retained, the Real Presence was recognised and Lenten fasting was enjoined. Little bullying of the clergy by the civil government was needed to secure the changes. Two things, in themselves moderate, may have held radical implications since they struck at the roots of any idea that the laity were not fully part of the Church. One was the insistence that the Canon of the Mass, the central portion of the service, was no longer to be recited *sotto voce*. The other was of course the English Prayer Book.

At first a few ignorant and obscurantist peasants disliked the Prayer Book, calling it a mummery or " a Christmas game ". Perhaps there had been a magical property in the Latin words they could not understand. But the Prayer Book soon won the victories that it deserved. It secured for the congregation an integral share in the worship of God and an opportunity to take an intelligent interest in what was going on. It was a miracle of English prose composition, not least because the prose is varied according to requirement, ranging from the evocative prose-poetry of Coverdale's psalms to the classical and exact economy of Cranmer's collects.

The Prayer Book was to survive with remarkably little change, all the vicissitudes and religious upheavals of the next hundred years. Its quiet decency and dignity were to do more than any other single factor to set the peculiar tones and overtones of Anglican religion. It was to win the passionate loyalties of generations of men. It was to enrol martyrs in its cause. Indeed it was mainly for the Prayer

Book that the King and the Cavaliers fought and failed, since we cannot easily suppose that men ventured their lives for the sake of government by bishops. The Prayer Book cadences rolled on sonorously until in 1928 this well of English undefiled was poisoned by a clique of clergymen, and the Anglican church-goer lost his birthright of listening to great prose.

The Prayer Book remained capable of bearing " Catholic " interpretations. Nothing in fact in the book of 1549 was anything other than a direct translation of some older piece of liturgy. Nevertheless, by lifting the censorship, by authorising Cranmer's *Homilies* some of which had Protestant implications, and above all by inviting to England a number of foreign Protestant intellectuals, Somerset did much towards making England eventually Protestant. The coming of the foreigners is doubly significant. Had there been enough native Protestants of light and learning there would have been no need to call in the German Bucer, the Italian Peter Martyr or the Pole John à Lasco, all of whom were given university posts and were much consulted. Henry VIII had rushed through his anti-Papal measures so fast that it might almost be said that there was an English Reformation before there was any considerable body of English Reformers. It is clear also that, in the eyes of the government, to adopt the Protestant religion meant joining the Protestant " International " abroad. There was as yet nothing insular or provincial about it. Protestantism was conceived of as a league of reformed Catholic Churches, purged of Italianate corruptions and returning to the path once trodden by the Fathers.

There is no evidence that Somerset intended his Prayer Book as an interim measure or meant to push the Reformation further. That his successor did go further proves nothing about the plans of Somerset. Nor is there any evidence that Somerset had Calvinist sympathies, as some of his enemies averred. His Prayer Book lent no support to Calvinist eucharistic views and he showed no signs of

wishing to abolish bishops. It seems that he had vaguely
" Protestant " opinions of a general kind and was enough of
a realist to see that England had reached a point of no
return. Certainly he was enough of a patriot not to regret
it. He replied in resolute words when Pole proposed sub-
mitting the religious settlement to a synod of " indifferent
men ". How could any friend of Pole's, he asked, be " indifferent " on the subject of the Pope's supremacy? " For
our parts, that are true Englishmen and faithful subjects
to the King's Majesty, we suppose there is no one indifferent
man in that point. And we would be sorry there should;
but we will all live and die in his Highness' quarrel; and
sooner spend all our lives and goods than his Majesty
should lose of his regality and imperial power one jot. . . .
If we knew any such indifferent man as you speak on in the
King's Majesty's realm, it should not be long before he
should have as he deserveth. And if we should forswear and
neglect our duties therein the common people would pluck
him in pieces, to whom the name of the Pope is as odious
as the name of the devil himself."[28] We can see in Somerset's patriotic anti-papalism some faint foreshadowing of
that nineteenth-century attitude which was to look on the
Catholic Church as " the Italian mission to England ".

Dudley, soon to be Duke of Northumberland, pushed
further out into the Protestant stream, but from much less
reputable motives. Almost certainly he had in mind the
eventual abolition of episcopacy, so as to squeeze the last
drops out of ecclesiastical property. To pass some of his
measures he dispensed with the consent of Convocation
and, exploiting the king's own Protestant zeal, even by-
passed the consent of the Council. Nor did he work in
harmony with all of the Protestant divines. Cranmer was
not allowed to put into force his great reform of the Canon
Law, because it might have preserved some vestiges of
self-government for the Church. Latimer and Lever fell
out of favour because they had preached that rich men had
obligations to the poor. Knox, who was sounded for a

bishopric, was found to have too much a mind of his own and to be "neither grateful nor pleasable".

There were some more pliant and unscrupulous clergy who proved quite willing to toe Dudley's line since there were pickings to be had, even for clergymen, out of ecclesiastical spoils. Such were the Dean and two Canons of Chester who were later imprisoned for stripping off and selling their own cathedral's lead. Dudley's lay supporters included Sir Philip Hoby, Master of the Ordnance, who had a project for endowing a crack cavalry regiment with some confiscated episcopal wealth.

It is remarkable that Dudley came so near to success, with so few real friends, with such disreputable support and with so many obvious opponents. But he had the backing of some Protestant fanatics and of the more blatantly avaricious of the "new men". He had a little clandestine French support, since France feared Spanish influence in England if Mary became queen. Dudley had, too, a certain popularity as the most successful soldier in the country. He had his extraordinary personal ascendancy over the king. And he possessed real genius for political manoeuvre. "He had," said Sir Richard Morison, "such a head that he seldom went about anything but he conceived first three or four purposes beforehand", meaning perhaps three or four alternative plans, or conceivably three or four double bluffs.[29]

Above all, Dudley had an immensely strong and indeed almost terrifying personality. When he summoned the judges to suborn them into declaring legal Lady Jane Grey's succession to the throne, some of them were hesitant, notably Chief Justice Sir Edward Montagu. According to Montague, Dudley was "in a great rage and fury, trembling for anger, and amongst his ragious talk called the said Sir Edward traitor; and further said that he would fight in his shirt with any man in that quarrel". Montagu was in "dread then that the Duke would have stricken one of them". The king, too, addressed the judges "with sharp words and angry countenance ", so that Montagu was " in great fear as ever he was in his life before, seeing the King so earnest and sharp and the Duke so angry. . . . who ruled the whole Council as it pleased him ".[80]

Nevertheless the dice were loaded against Dudley. The majority of Englishmen were still, in some sense, Catholic in religious feeling; and a very great majority were certainly unwilling to see King Henry's eldest daughter lose her birthright. We must remember that Catherine of Aragon had never ceased to be popular. Besides, most Englishmen feared France more than Spain. Dudley's Protestant reforms had been too rapid, too drastic and too patently cynical to win much popularity. The economic situation had not improved. Nothing had been done to reform the currency. Prices were still rising, and any attempt by the government to fix maximum prices only resulted in driving commodities off the market altogether. As Sir John Mason wrote to Secretary Cecil in December 1550, " Ever the end is dearth and lack of the thing we seek to make ' good cheap '. Nature will have her course . . . and never shall you drive her to consent that a pennyworth shall be sold for a farthing."[81]

Nor had Dudley many real friends even in the Council. He found it necessary to visit the king by night, so as not to be seen by colleagues who were jealous of his influence. He also found it more and more necessary to by-pass the Council and proceed by authority of the king alone. Lord Chancellor Rich resigned in protest; and the departure of so notorious a rat may be taken as a sign that Dudley's ship was sinking.

The scheme to make Lady Jane Grey Edward's heiress was so shameless that it had little chance of success. Ostensibly, the rights of Mary and Elizabeth were passed over on the grounds that the kingdom could not be entrusted to female rule; and both of them might conceivably be thought bastards. But at the last moment the words in the " Device " giving the succession to " the heirs male " of

Lady Jane were changed to "the Lady Jane *and* her heirs male", thus openly making another female heir-apparent to the throne. This inconsistency, combined with forgery, was forced on Dudley because it had become clear that Edward would die before Lady Jane could have any heirs.

In January 1553 Edward began to have "a tough, strong, straining cough", followed by "a weakness and faintness of spirit".[32] It was probably acute pulmonary tuberculosis. By the end of May he was "steadily pining away. He does not sleep except he be stuffed with drugs. . . . The sputum which he brings up is livid, black, fetid and full of carbon; it smells beyond measure. . . . His feet are swollen all over. To the doctors all these things portend death, and that within three months." So wrote John Banister, a young medical student attached to the royal household.[33] On July 6th the boy died, praying (we are told) with his last breath, "Lord God, deliver me out of this miserable wretched life"; and also "O Lord God, save thy chosen people of England. O my Lord God, defend this realm from papistry, and maintain Thy true religion."[34]

The prayer may not be a mere literary fabrication, intended to edify and supposedly appropriate to "the young Josiah"; for one of the things that is most certain about Edward is his obdurate Protestantism. A little earlier the Council, fearing diplomatic and military pressure from Charles V, had tried to persuade the king to wink at his sister Mary's private masses. Edward asked them if they could prove that the scripture was idolatry was ever to be tolerated. He would not, he said, "set light God's will, thereby to please an Emperor". It was not a liberal sentiment but it sounds a note of wilfulness and of defiance that is unmistakably Tudor.

CHAPTER VI

MARY TUDOR

1553-1558

In August 1551 a deputation of Councillors had called on the Princess Mary at Copt Hall, in Essex. Their business was to insist that at long last divine worship in her household should conform to the Prayer Book ordained by law. The princess was ill and isolated, and she had suffered more than twenty years of humiliation and insult. She had known of Anne Boleyn's intrigues against her life. She could remember two Queens of England going to the block and, knowing the character of those about the young king, she cannot have supposed that the life of a princess was *ipso facto* safe. But she did not prevaricate. She protested her willingness to obey the king " in any thing, her conscience saved ". But rather than " use any other service than was used at the death of the late king, her father, she would lay her head on a block and suffer death; but (said she) I am unworthy to suffer death in so good a quarrel ". She made a shrewd hit when she said that, although Edward, " good sweet King, have more knowledge than any other of his years, yet it is not possible that he can be a judge in these things ". It was not to be supposed that at fourteen Edward was yet competent to command a naval expedition. " Much less . . . can he in these years discern what is fittest in matters of divinity."

If her chaplains, for fear of punishment, refused to say Mass for her, even so " none of your new service . . . shall be used in my house ". Naturally she unsheathed her only weapon, the protection of her cousin the Emperor Charles V. " Though you esteem little the Emperor," she said, " yet should you show more favour to me for my father's sake, who made the more part of you out of nothing." The hit was palpable and fair enough. "As for the Emperor . . . if he were dead I would say as I do; and if he would give me now other advice I would not follow it." She could not resist adding, "Notwithstanding, to be plain to you, his ambassador shall know how I am used at your hands . . . I will not die willingly, but will do the best I can to preserve my life; but if I shall chance to die, I will protest openly that you of the Council be the causes of my death; you give me fair words, but your deeds be always ill towards me." Without any whining or loss of dignity she made one request, that she might be given back the controller of her household; for, since his departure, she had had to keep her own accounts "and learn how many loaves of bread be made of a bushel of wheat, and I wis my father and mother never brought me up to baking and brewing, and, to be plain with you, I am weary of mine office; and, therefore, if my Lords will send mine officer home, they shall do me pleasure; otherwise if they will send him to prison, I be-shrew him if he go not to it merrily, and with a good will." It was as if Lear had anticipated the stocking of his servant.

The princess had one parting shot—"And I pray God to send you well to do in your souls and bodies too, for some of you have but weak bodies."[1] If her hearers were sensitive they must have noted two recurring motifs in her speech— the harping upon her father's stature and the uncompromising candour that emerges in the phrase "to be plain with you" which she kept slipping in.

A month later Ridley, Bishop of London, called on her at Hunsdon, in Hertfordshire. "Madam," he said, "I trust you will not refuse God's Word." She answered, "I cannot tell what ye call God's Word; that is not God's Word now that was God's Word in my father's days." "God's Word," replied Ridley, "is all one in all times, but hath been better understood and practised in some ages than others." But

Mary was not to be so easily put down. " You durst not for your ears have avouched that for God's Word in my father's days that now you do. And, as for your new books, I thank God I never read any of them; I never did, nor ever will do." She ended by saying, " My Lord, for your gentleness to come and see me, I thank you; but for your offering to preach before me, I thank you never a whit."[2] No one but a Tudor ever spoke in words of such a kind.

Mary indeed had all the family courage and all the family stubbornness. What she had not was the ability, so marked in other Tudors, to throw high principle to the winds. She was the only adult Tudor who was upright, the only adult Tudor with a genuine conscience. It is her tragedy and it is an irony of history that she was the only Tudor who failed and the only Tudor who did her country indisputable harm.

It is strange that Mary spoke of her father with such apparent respect. He had made her a bastard, reduced her mother to the utmost misery, threatened at moments her own life and treated her with such meanness that she was not even allowed to visit her dying mother nor to inherit the furs her mother left her. But Henry had been every inch a king, and there must have been something in that which struck a resonance within her character. It was to be the same with Elizabeth who had also been slighted as a child by Henry and whose mother he had actually killed.

Perhaps Mary remembered that in happier days she had given her father cause for pride. In May 1527, when she was just eleven, she had taken part in a pageant at Greenwich for the entertainment of foreign ambassadors. She had dazzled the company by her dancing, " decked with all the gems of the eighth sphere "; and afterwards the king had taken off her cap and her hair-net to display her " profusion of silver tresses as beautiful as ever seen on human head "—in the opinion of the Venetian secretary.[3] Even four years later, when her mother had fallen, Henry was still reported to be treating Mary with affection. He may still have liked her " pretty face and . . . very beautiful complexion ", her diminutive but " well-proportioned physique ". She was delicate but her looks were not yet marred by the ill-health which became almost chronic before she was twenty. Besides, the king may have liked to show off her accomplishments—she spoke Spanish, French and Latin, could read Greek and Italian, sang well and played on several instruments.[4] And she was still, after all, Henry's only legitimate heir. Her humiliations began only after the birth of Elizabeth (September 7th, 1533).

In spite of frequent toothache leading to the loss of many teeth, in spite of palpitations of the heart, in spite of headaches and depression consequent upon amenorrhoea, in spite of all her mental sufferings, she was still, at the age of thirty-seven in the first year of her reign, not altogether soured; nor were her charms entirely faded. Soranzo the Venetian Ambassador found her " of low stature, with a red and white complexion, and very thin ". Her eyes were large and pale (" bianchi "), her hair reddish. He noticed also the flattened nose seen in her portraits. Yet he thought that " were not her age on the decline, she might be called handsome (' bella ') rather than the contrary."[5] He also records that " Her Majesty's countenance indicates great benignity and clemency, which are not belied by her conduct ". This was true, for she had just startled her counsellors by pardoning all but the ring-leaders of Northumberland's conspiracy, and had indeed been dissuaded with some difficulty from pardoning Lady Jane Grey herself.

The Venetian was impressed by the queen's almost puritanical way of life. " She is of very spare diet, and never eats until 1 or 2 p.m., although she rises at daybreak when, after saying her prayers and hearing Mass in private, she transacts business incessantly until after midnight, when she retires to rest; for she chooses to give audience, not only to all the members of her Privy Council, and to hear from them every detail of public business, but also to all other persons who ask it of her ". The only indulgences she allowed herself, he thought, were the wearing of fine clothes and " great use of jewels . . . in which she delights greatly, and although she has a great plenty of them left her by her predecessors, yet were she better supplied with money than she is, she would doubtless buy many more."[6]

She had always been staid and demure, and so virtuous as to be not a little innocent. According to one of her maids of honour, Jane Dormer, Mary was " so bred as she . . . knew no foul or unclean speeches, which when her Lord Father understood, he would not believe it ". Characteristically, Henry is said to have induced the courtier Sir Francis Bryan to test Mary's virtue at a masque by using improper language which she completely failed to understand.[7]

Her innocence persisted for, within two years of her death, she overheard the Lord Chamberlain, " a merry gentleman ", flirting with Frances Neville, a maid of honour, chucking her under the chin and saying " My pretty——, how dost thou?" The queen shortly afterwards made use of the same gesture and expression, to the horror of her maid, who had to explain, " My Lord Chamberlain is an idle gentleman, and we respect not what he saith or doth; but your Majesty from whom I think I never heard any such word, doth amaze me, either in jest or earnest, to be called so by you. A —— is a wicked misliving woman." " Thou must forgive me," said the queen, " for I meant thee no harm."[8] We do not know which unseemly word was used. Jane Dormer's Victorian editor thought it would " not bear repetition ".

There may well have been more than the conventional flattery of a hanger-on in the poem called *A Description of a Most Noble Lady*, written by John Heywood who was for many years Mary's semi-official laureate and entertainer. The poem, composed when the princess was eighteen, celebrates her beauty in the usual manner—to the point of crudity—

> Give place, ye ladies! all be gone;
>   Show not yourselves at all.
> For why? behold! there cometh one
>   Whose face yours all blank shall.

Yet there is a more sincere note in the references to her moral qualities.

> In life a Dian chaste;
>   In truth Penelope;
> In word and deed steadfast—
>   What need I more to say?
> At Bacchus' feast none may her meet;
>   Or yet at any wanton play;
> Nor gazing in the open street,
>   Or wandering as astray.

> The mirth that she doth use
>   Is mixed with shamefastness;
> All vices she eschews,
>   And hateth idleness.[9]

"Steadfast" she remained all her life, particularly in her religion. Soranzo recalls that she constantly muttered to herself "*In te Domine confido, non confundar in aeternum: si Deus est pro nobis, quis contra nos?*"[10] It is curious, perhaps prophetic, that her first recorded utterance was the word "Priest". She was two years old and, on being brought into her father's presence before various grandees, she caught sight of Dionysio Memo, the king's Venetian organist and chaplain. "The Princess," we are told, "began calling out in English 'Priest!' and he was obliged to play for her."[11]

Music she never ceased to love. It was one of the things, like her delight in finery, which show her to have been not wholly other-worldly or "inhuman". Another was her fondness for small children. There can be little doubt that she had a pathetically thwarted maternal instinct. Even the small Elizabeth, whose very existence was her elder sister's greatest injury, won Mary's affection by her childish precocity. She was " such a child toward ", Mary wrote to her father, " as I doubt not your Highness shall have cause to rejoice of in time coming, as knoweth Almighty God."[12] For a time too, until religion separated them, Mary had bestowed kindness and affection on her baby brother Edward. Years later, she held up her own wedding preparations for several hours in order to choose a name and suitable god-parents for the new-born child of Noailles, the French Ambassador (with whom she had not always been on the best of terms), giving up, wrote Noailles, " more patience and time than I would have asked in four good audiences."[13]

There is much evidence of Mary's natural kindliness. When she was queen she used to visit poor families near Croydon, dressed indistinguishably from her attendants so as not to be recognised, in order to see how the poor lived, to redress their grievances and, sometimes, to provide apprenticeships for their children.[14] She left provision in her will for what would have been the first English hospital for disabled soldiers, if Queen Elizabeth had not ignored the bequest.[15] Nor was Mary's goodness merely priggish. She liked her pleasures and her games. She was rebuked by her truly priggish little brother for excessive dancing. She spent over £2000 in salaries alone on music and drama in the first year of her reign.[16] Even when she was a princess living on very short commons, she could lose ten shillings, the price of a " breakfast ", wagered on a game of bowls,[17] as well as numerous sums over cards. Royal wagering was of course common form, and Mary never approached her father's expenditure of over £3000 in the course of three years on bets lost at cards, dice, hunting, tennis and other games.[18]

She respected literary talent and made Roger Ascham, despite his Protestantism, her Latin secretary. Such was the

queen's liking for dramatic entertainment that she overlooked the anti-clerical squibs which her protégé John
Heywood put into his Interludes; and she actually made
Nicholas Udall headmaster of Westminster, out of respect
for his learning and for his gifts as a comic playwright,
although he had written Protestant propaganda and
although he had lost the headmastership of Eton for having
purloined the college plate and for having fallen under suspicion of even graver improprieties. As a princess, Mary
had made many payments to " Jane the Fool " and to
" Lucretia the Tumbler ".

Mary might so easily have made a model sovereign in the
Tudor pattern. She had virtue, courage, dignity, learning,
intelligence and considerable charm. Her accession was
greeted by the people with even greater joy than they had
shown when her father became king. Never had London
known such throwing up of caps, such casting of money out
of windows, such bonfires and banqueting in the streets,
" such shouting and crying of the people, and ringing of
bells, there could no one man hear almost what another
said ".[19] Mary showed herself generous in victory and she
gave no sign of kicking over any constitutional traces. She
told her judges to allow prisoners their full legal rights :
" You are to sit there, not as advocates for me, but as
indifferent judges between me and my people." And she
is said to have thrown into the fire a scheme of the Imperial
Ambassador's to set up an English despotism.[20] She did not
hurry unduly in reversing her predecessor's religious policy,
unpopular though much of it had been. She did not use
unconstitutional machinery. She did not seriously press her
hope of restoring the abbey lands. Yet, after reigning no
more than five years, she died hated and an utter failure.
Once more " all the churches in London did ring, and at
night [men] did make bonfires and set tables in the street,
and did eat and drink, and make merry, for the new
queen ".[21]

If honesty had been the best policy Mary would certainly

have succeeded, for she made no bones about her intentions. She never lacked the courage of her convictions, nor indeed any other sort of courage. It was her obvious gallantry in the opening days of her reign which rallied so many waverers to the standard she set up at Framlingham when Northumberland, the best soldier of the day, had reached Cambridge on his march against her.

A few months later the rebel Wyatt was at Ludgate and the London trained bands had deserted to him rather than " be under the rule of the proud Spaniards or strangers ". Mary refused to leave the City for Windsor. She refused to employ the brave Egmont and other Imperial envoys who offered their services. She refused to bombard the rebels in Southwark from the Tower, for fear of killing innocent civilians. At the Guildhall she made a speech which, in all probability, turned the tide. The speech, " which she seemed to have perfectly conned, without book ", was brave, simple, frank, quite uncompromising and supremely effective. " What I am," she said, " ye right well know. I am your Queen, to whom at my coronation, when I was wedded to the realm and the laws of the same . . . you promised your allegiance. . . . My father, as ye all know, possessed the same regal state, which now rightly is descended unto me; and to him always ye showed yourselves most faithful and loving subjects; and therefore I doubt not but ye will show yourselves likewise unto me. . . . I cannot tell how naturally the mother loveth a child, for I was never the mother of any, but certainly if a prince and governor may as naturally and earnestly love her subjects as the mother doth love her child, then assure yourselves that I . . . do as earnestly and tenderly love and favour you. And I . . . cannot but think that ye as heartily and faithfully love me; and then I doubt not but that we shall give these rebels a short and speedy overthrow."

As to her marriage, she said, she would not for " mine own pleasure . . . choose where I lust ", nor was she " so desirous " that she needed a husband. " For God I thank

Him . . . I have hitherto lived a virgin, and doubt nothing but that with God's grace I am able so to live still. But if, as my progenitors have done before me, it may please God that I might leave some fruit of my body behind me to be your governor, I trust you would not only rejoice thereat but also I know it would be to your great comfort. . . . And on the word of a Queen, I promise you, that if it shall not probably appear to all the nobility and commons . . . that this marriage shall be for the high benefit and commodity of the realm, then I will abstain from marriage while I live. And now, good subjects, pluck up your hearts, and like true men, stand fast against these rebels . . . and fear them not, for, I assure you, I fear them nothing at all."[22] Except for a certain prolixity, her words are not inferior to Queen Elizabeth's Armada speech.

Yet there were many reasons for Mary's failure. She was ill-starred almost from her birth. No woman had ruled England for the last four centuries, and Mary's sex was enough in itself to present her with unmanageable problems. A woman was expected to lean upon male counsellors. A woman was hardly honourable if she did not marry. And a queen must have an heir if she wishes her policy continued or if her country is to avoid a disputed succession. Yet Mary was almost too old to have children. At thirty-seven she was, by the standards of the time, almost more than middle-aged. Time, indeed, had not been on her side. Illness and suffering had removed the feminine charms that she might once have exploited. Ten years earlier she would have been a much more eligible bride and she might have made her sex a political and diplomatic weapon, as her sister was to do with such triumphant skill. Ten years earlier, too, she might have stopped the English Reformation in its tracks; but by now it had developed too much impetus. It had enlisted many poor men's devotion and many rich men's interest.

The fault, however, did not lie wholly in Mary's stars. She had her own limitations. Renard, the Imperial Ambassador, found her "easily influenced, inexpert in worldly matters and a novice all round"; and he feared that she would be undone "either by the machinations of the French" or else "by the conspiracies of the English". Above all, he feared the "enchantments" of the Princess Elizabeth who had, he said "*un esprit plein d'incantation*".[23] It is indeed more than possible that Mary was undone by her clemency to Elizabeth. The princess, merely by existing, gave the opposition a focus and a hope. But Mary was obstinately merciful. There is evidence that either she or Gardiner deliberately mislaid some intercepted dispatches which implicated Elizabeth both in Wyatt's rebellion and in intrigues with the French.[24] It is arguable that Mary was too hard over religious matters and too soft over political. She might well have succeeded had she burnt less heretics but beheaded more traitors.

Probably she was not too good a judge of men; but, unless she was to make a clean sweep of all the experienced administrators and politicians in the country, she had only a shady set of men from which to choose. Almost all of them had something sinister in their past and were at least half committed to the *status quo*. Most were double dealers and most were jealous of the others. The great majority of her bishops were worldlings who had toed her father's ecclesiastical line; and if they now thought the time had come for a return to Rome, it was very possibly because Edward's reign had shown that heterodoxy in religion opened the way to social and political disorders which they found rather more disturbing.[25] Gardiner, the ablest of them, had much to live down. He is reported to have said himself on his death-bed that he had denied with Peter but had not yet wept with Peter. He had written anti-Papal propaganda for Henry, admittedly out of fear. Since then, however, he had gone to the Tower under Edward. His imprisonment had aged him prematurely, and he was now a wise and moderate, though not a strong man. In any case he had not long to live.

After Gardiner, Mary unfortunately turned to Reginald Pole. It is not surprising, for on paper he had everything to recommend him. He was of royal blood. He too had seen an innocent mother, the Countess of Salisbury (once Mary's governess), fall a victim to Henry's brutal tyranny. He had been a possible Pope and a possible King of England. He had always denounced the Reformers without ceasing to advocate sober ecclesiastical reform. He had an international reputation for learning, wisdom, moderation. He was a scholar, a gentleman and a saint. He had unquestioned integrity and he had immense personal charm. *Omnium consensu capax imperii nisi imperasset.*

But Pole had been out of England for nearly a quarter of a century and was hopelessly out of touch with the realities of the English situation. It might be said that he hardly knew what the English Reformation was all about. He was also, to Mary's bitter grief, by no means *persona grata* with the reigning Pope, the stern and irascible Paul IV. Pole had, moreover, become prolix in controversy and stiff and wooden in his opinions. He was, in fact, a thin-lipped, bloodless, priggish intellectual. He had, it is true, great experience in diplomacy but this had only given him a " Foreign Office " mind, an unshakable but quite unrealistic belief that all problems could be solved at the conference table, provided that tempers were kept and good manners observed and provided that only moderate men attended. He refused to see Cranmer or any deep-dyed heretic in person. He handled most things with kid gloves and often seemed oblivious of what was going on. He did not desire persecution but did nothing effective to prevent it. He produced a grandiose scheme to purify the English Church and did little to get it carried out. When he was needed to give practical advice he was apt to be found at his private devotions or engaged in pious and refined discourse with cultivated friends. He had a fatal lack of humour and could not see that no good could come of the public burning of

dead heretics' exhumed remains, though it might give him
the satisfaction of feeling that he was relatively humane.
He had, too, an un-English propensity for hitting a man
when he was down and insisted on adding lengthy passages
to the recantations of Cranmer and of Cheke, so as to make
them yet more abject. Above all, Pole, like Mary, got his
chance too late. He was already old and tired, and he only
outlived the queen by twelve hours.

If Pole did little good in Mary's cause, her marriage with
the Prince of Spain did positive harm. Probably it came too
late to do her the only good it might have done, that is, by
ensuring her an heir. It never had any chance of proving
popular and was in fact a major blunder, though it was
understandable enough. Almost from her infancy Mary's
hand had been hawked around Europe and offered to every
prince from Portugal to Poland. But for a princess who was
dubbed a bastard by her own father the bidding had been
inevitably low. Naturally she felt humiliated; and naturally
the Spanish match, the grandest in all Europe, could do
something to restore her proper pride. She knew, of course,
that all her plans would founder if she had no heir. She
knew also that her heir would have enemies at home and
abroad; and she could give him no stronger backing against
them than the fabulous wealth and power of the Hapsburgs.
Apart from all this, we cannot discount her genuine, human
love of children. It is also possible that, like other Tudors,
she was not undersexed.

How far and in what sense Mary was in love with Philip
we cannot know. She may have persuaded herself that she
loved the man. She was almost certainly in love with what
he represented—the prospect of a Catholic heir, reunion
with Rome, her martyred mother's Spanish dynasty, the
Spain that stood for centuries of knight-errantry against the
infidel. He was the rising hope and appointed champion of
Catholic unity; he seemed to embody an old-world romantic
Christian chivalry; he had about him—for her—gleams and

glints of the lost, stately, European culture which Henry VIII had thrown away in exchange for raw, insular, complacent barbarism.

But Mary's chosen knight-errant was to prove imperfect and ungentle. Philip was outwardly correct, punctilious and attentive as a husband. But his whole temperament was cold and scheming. With his intimates he dropped all pretence that the marriage was anything more to him than a political convenience. It is probable that he had already given to a Spanish lady what heart he ever possessed. He is also alleged to have complained that the painters of Mary's portraits had flattered her to deceive him. Before long he was rumoured to be over-familiar with ladies of the court, to be seducing baker's daughters and even to be flirting with Elizabeth as an insurance for keeping the English alliance after Mary's death. Spaniards on the continent were saying openly and brutally, " What shall the king do with such an old bitch?" and that the queen was old enough to be his mother—actually she was ten years his senior. An English Protestant pamphleteer even attributed to Philip himself the remark that " The baker's daughter is better in her gown than Queen Mary without the crown ", though it is doubtful whether Philip knew English well enough to be capable of such rhyming.[26]

Politically the match was a disaster. Henry VIII had done nothing if he had not made his country insular; and the queen's projected union with a foreigner was unpopular from the outset. Wyatt's rebellion was the immediate result. The Council was only persuaded with great difficulty and the Commons lodged a protest. Mary had to address them in the accents later to be used so frequently by Elizabeth upon matrimonial matters. Parliament, Mary said, was "not accustomed to use such language to the Kings of England " and as to her marriage " she would choose as God inspired her ".[27]

The nation's misgiving was well grounded. Spain got much the better of the bargain, dragging England unprofitably into the Hapsburg quarrel with France and even into the Hapsburg quarrel with the Pope. Philip intrigued to make himself more than a Prince Consort. Attempts were made to introduce Spanish methods of government and inquisitorial procedure. Spaniards and Englishmen came to blows within the purlieus of the court. And Englishmen were not allowed to break into Spanish monopolies in the New World trade. If Mary died hated by her subjects, it was as much due to the Spanish marriage as it was to her religious persecution.

Nor did the marriage bring Mary any personal happiness. Philip did take the trouble, at any rate in public, to use "love-talk" to her. But he seems to have told at least one Spanish confidant that he found her unattractive, lacking "all sensibility of the flesh", thin in the wrong places, without eyebrows and, by Spanish standards, badly dressed. One young Spaniard recorded indelicately that "it would take God himself to drink of this cup".[28] As soon as diplomacy and decency allowed him, Philip left her. The baby Mary longed for and so genuinely believed to have quickened was in fact never conceived. She was misled by some dropsy or tumour near the womb.

Philip left her with another responsibility upon her hands, for he had been most careful not to let himself be associated with her policy towards heretics. This was certainly not due to clemency, for Philip's first act when he returned to Spain was to attend an *auto-da-fé* and see fourteen people burned. Besides, Mary was to burn some three hundred heretics in the course of three years, whereas during half of that same period the Spaniards executed thirteen hundred heretics in the Province of Holland alone.[29] The explanation is that Philip, acting on his father the Emperor's advice, was afraid of the political consequences of persecution in England and was anxious not to court unpopularity for Spain. Even before any persecution began, the Spanish friars who came to Winchester for the royal wedding had to stay inside the College, since they

T.   E were not safe from the mob if they appeared in the streets.

The responsibility for persecution must be shared between Queen Mary and her advisers, both lay and clerical. To the queen herself it must have seemed that there was no other way of restoring England to the Church. The stake was the inevitable corollary of her religious views. She may have thought when she began that a few prominent examples would suffice for her purpose. But cruelty, as twentieth-century Europe has cause to know, is highly infectious and, once let loose, not easily restrained. In any case Mary would have found it hard to spare Cranmer, who had not only pronounced Henry and Anne Boleyn man and wife, but had been deeply involved in Northumberland's projects. Mary may not have known that Cranmer had once interceded with Henry to save her from the block when she refused to renounce the Pope's supremacy.[30] It might, however, have been better policy to behead Cranmer as a traitor than to make him a martyr for his religious views. The people were used to treason trials, and the game of politics was recognised to be a dangerous one which a man played with his life as the forfeit. Yet Mary preferred it to be thought that Cranmer's offence was not against herself but against God and Holy Church. He had put the souls of Englishmen in mortal peril and had been the prime mover in national apostacy. Such enormities could be purged by fire alone.

In any case it would not have been easy to bring home a charge of treason against most of the Protestants. In the opening days of her reign Mary owed much to the fleet which was full of Protestants but declared for her at once, as had Colchester and Yarmouth, perhaps the most Protestant towns outside London. Among her earliest supporters had been Bishop Hooper, whom she sent to the stake within a year. When Wyatt was approaching London he offered to release the Protestant prisoners in the Marshalsea but they told him that " as we came in for our consciences, and [were] sent hither by the Council, we think it good here still to remain till it please God to work our deliverance as it shall seem best to His Glory and our lawful discharge; whether it be life or death we are content, His will be done upon us! and thus fare you well."[31] The Protestant doctrine of non-resistance could go no further.

It can at least be said that Cranmer and Hooper and the other divines who suffered were clearly guilty under Catholic law and received trials which were technically more or less scrupulous and fair. They did not suffer, as so many of Henry's victims had done, simply because the sovereign disliked or feared them, or because they had given the sovereign bad advice. Yet they would not have suffered if their sovereign had not willed it. Mary cannot be acquitted of her personal share in the responsibility. She discouraged Pole from showing any leniency.[32] She rebuked Bonner for delaying his proceedings against heresy.[33] Perhaps it was less amiable still that she should have reprimanded the Sheriff of Hampshire for sparing a heretic who had recanted at the first touch of the flame.[34]

The Council, doubtless, played a big part in the decision to persecute : and they may not have been disinterested, for many of their own number could easily have been accused of former *treasons*. By directing the queen's wrath into ecclesiastical channels they may have been saving their own skins. Some of them could equally well have been charged with former heresies; but one was allowed to repent of one's former heresies and live, whereas the repentant traitor went to the block just the same. What is certain is that the Council could have stopped the persecution if they had wished. As Philip's Spanish companions noted, " the people who really govern are the Councillors; . . . and they are feared much more than the Sovereign ".[35] The Council and Parliament made it quite clear that they would not tolerate the restoration of the abbey lands. Nor did they want the queen to drop either in fact or in name the Royal Supremacy over the Church. They showed on more than one occasion that they were not frightened of stormy debates with the sovereign. They could, therefore, had they wished, have dug in their toes about the persecution.

It is highly significant that none of the rich and great laymen who were the really interested parties, the real power behind the English Reformation, went to the stake. Those who did were a few eminent Protestant divines, and a large number of poor, humble, very simple persons. Some may have been fanatics and some half-crazed but the great majority were eminently harmless. A few were guilty of violence against priests or of ribald outrages against the Mass. A few could be accused of Anabaptism, that is, of taking literally and seriously the Gospel teaching upon war and property, an attitude which has always been profoundly shocking to respectable persons. Cranmer and other Protestant Bishops had burned Anabaptists under earlier sovereigns, though only in extreme cases and in very small numbers.

It was natural in the sixteenth century to think of religion as the bond which held society together and to realise that a man who differed from his sovereign over religion must almost inevitably desire a different sovereign. It was impossible for Tudor minds to make our dichotomy between religion and politics. Heresy was a civil as well as an ecclesiastical offence, and treason was both crime and sin. Nor, of course, were Tudor minds beset by any squeamishness about the infliction of physical pain, although we must remember that in Tudor England torture was uncommon and not fully legal.

That there should have been burnings, then, we can readily understand. What is less easily understandable is the selection of the victims. Almost all the ring-leaders among the laity and many among the divines were allowed to pass into exile, unmolested and unhurried. The Duchess of Suffolk took five weeks to reach Gravesend from London and was accompanied by a retinue that included a major-domo, a brewer, a kitchen-maid, a laundress, a Greek "rider of horses" and a fool—although they were called "the meanest of her servants ".[36] Some of the exiles even received government passports and were allowed letters of credit to transfer their wealth overseas. Sir John Cheke, it is true, was later kidnapped and brought to England after he had shown himself to be the chief Protestant propagandist. He was threatened with the stake and recanted in an abject and pathetic manner. Yet Sir Peter Carew (who was arrested with him) was soon released, although he had tried to raise Devonshire against the Spanish marriage and from his exile had been privateering against Spanish ships. It is possible however that Sir Peter had bought his freedom by betraying Cheke.[37]

What is striking in the persecution is the number of victims, between fifty and sixty in all, who were women. It is hard to believe that many of them were very dangerous characters. There were, for example, the four Essex women who "could not tell what a sacrament is" or how many sacraments there were. One of the women, "a young maid unskilled . . . had heard that there was one sacrament, but what it was she could not tell". Another was technically a relapsed Catholic, though she had been taught nothing but the Protestant faith since she was eleven, "in King Edward's day". She cannot have been more than eighteen when she was burned. Nor is it likely that Thomas Drowry, the blind boy of Gloucester, had greatly imperilled the salvation of his fellow mortals.[38] Still less can the nation's apostacy be blamed upon the Guernsey baby that was born while its mother Perotine Massey was being burned, and was itself thrown into the flames. The story was once thought an invention but has been proved true by modern scholarship.[39]

By Spanish or German standards there was little actual sadism, although there was something more than usually unpleasant about the burning of eleven men at three stakes in Stratford-atte-Bow, with two women "loose in the midst without any stake", to be roasted by a ring of fire.[40] It is perhaps to the credit of Marian England, though it did not benefit the martyrs, that many of the executioners were inexpert and bungled their work badly. Too often the faggots were damp and resulted in a cruelly slow fire, such as Hooper suffered though he had asked for a quick one, " shortly to make an end ". And there was Edward Horne of Newent who sang the 146th Psalm " until that his lips were burnt away."[41] Too often the gunpowder meant to provide a sudden death failed to explode, as in the case of Ridley who was fully conscious for three-quarters of an hour.

The English executioners failed to learn one important lesson from the Spanish Inquisition. In Spain the victims were usually gagged by the " agony pear " thrust into their mouths. This saved hypersensitive spectators from being discommoded by unpleasant noises. It also prevented the martyrs from making remarks, like Latimer's, that have echoed down the ages. A more competent and less humane Sheriff would have stopped Dr Rowland Taylor's mouth when he came to be burnt in his own parish of Hadleigh and alighted from his horse " and set a frisk or twain, as men commonly do in dancing. ' Why, Master Doctor,' quoth the Sheriff, ' How do you now?' He answered, ' Well, God be praised, good Master Sheriff. Never better : for now I know I am almost at home. I lack not past two stiles to go over, and I am even at my Father's house.' "[42] He was not, however, allowed to say anything but his prayers when he reached the stake. If Foxe is to be believed, the Council had threatened to cut out Taylor's tongue unless he promised this. He had indeed a dangerous tongue, for, as he was dressing for his execution, he hung for a moment by his hands from a beam in his cell, and said, " What a notable sway I should give if I were hanged ", meaning, wrote Foxe, " for that he was a corpulent and big man ".[48]

No wonder it became necessary for the Council to provide stronger guards at executions in order to stop men " comforting, aiding or praising the offender ", and to tell employers to see that their servants and apprentices were not at large at such times. More than once already the arrival of prisoners in London had turned into a triumphal procession.[44]

This was not due to any horror of religious persecution or of cruelty as such. It was almost certainly due to horror at persecution of the patently sincere by men whose past proclaimed them to be time-servers and " politiques ". There were, as the martyr Ralph Allerton told Bishop Bonner, three religions in England—" the first is that which you hold; the second is clean contrary to the same; and the third is a Neuter, being indifferent; that is to say, observing all things that are commanded outwardly as though he were of your part, his heart being set wholly against the same."[45]

The burnings indeed proved that there was in England a Protestant religion for which both learned divines and simple men and women, self-taught from the open Bible, were willing to die in torment. Until that had happened it might well have been thought that the only Protestants were either avaricious magnates greedy for Church lands or wild, undisciplined malcontents who hoped to overturn society. But it was now clear that Latimer's candle was alight in many honest consciences and that it could, in truth, never be put out. The Protestants had proved their sincerity and some of their persecutors were unable to free themselves from the suspicion of being " Neuters " conforming to the government's theology without great conviction.

Mary herself had few illusions about her own advisers. She is said to have told Philip that " when she looked around and carefully considered the persons about her she scarcely knew one who had not injured her, or who would fail to do so again if opportunity served ".[46]

A year before she died, Michiel the Venetian Ambassador found Mary prematurely aged, wrinkled by worries, very short-sighted with staring eyes and a " voice rough and loud, almost like a man's ". But she was still mentally alert and quick, still practising her musical instruments, still " courageous and resolute ", still preserving " a wonderful grandeur and dignity ". By now she had bitterly recognised that she would have no child; and the Venetian considered that she was maddened by the realisation that Elizabeth must inevitably succeed her.[47]

By the autumn of 1558 Mary was plainly very ill. Her end was hastened by some form of influenza. On November the 17th, after a long period of coma, she died. Once, when she came to, she told her women " what good dreams she had, seeing many little children like angels play before her, singing pleasing notes ".[48] After her death her prayer book was found to be much handled and tear-stained on those pages which set out the prayers for unity in the church and for women labouring with child.

CHAPTER VII

ELIZABETH THE FIRST

1558-1603

" The profusion of ornaments with which they are loaded," wrote Horace Walpole of Elizabeth's portraits, " are marks of her continual fondness for dress, while they entirely exclude all grace, and leave no more room for a painter's genius than if he had been employed to copy an Indian idol, totally composed of hands and necklaces. A pale Roman nose, a head of hair loaded with crowns and powdered with diamonds, a vast ruff, a vaster farthingale, and a bushel of pearls, are the features by which everybody knows at once the pictures of Elizabeth."[1]

Just the same trouble faces the historian. He is looking for a woman with the full allowance of flesh and blood that we should expect from a child of Henry VIII and of Anne Boleyn; and he is generally confronted with a wooden doll, a bundle of magnificent clothes and jewellery. " Her portraits," Froude complained, " are usually without shadow, as if her features radiated light . . . She is represented in more than mortal character."[2]

The painters were, perhaps unconsciously, obeying the queen's own behest; for she did her utmost to stylise herself, to constitute herself a legend. The demeanour of her court was stilted and mannered to a singular degree and was not rendered more natural by a studied and often coarse frivolity, by a false hilarity in which nicknames abounded, or by the elaborate make-believe of flirtation which had to be kept up long after it had lost all point or savour. It was all frankly vulgar.

> Go tell the court it glows
> And shines like rotten wood,

wrote the embittered Ralegh; and he was right, for into that court the fresh air never entered.

Yet Ralegh himself could succumb to the miasma. In 1592 he was capable of writing to a third party, Robert Cecil, in terms that are extravagant even for a courtier and even if we suppose that the queen was meant to see the letter. " My heart," he wrote, " was never broken till this day that I hear the Queen goes away so far off. . . . [I] am now left behind her in a dark prison all alone . . . I that was wont to behold her riding like Alexander, hunting like Diana, walking like Venus, the gentle wind blowing her fair hair about her pure cheeks like a nymph, sometime sitting in the shade like a goddess, sometime singing like an angel, sometime playing like Orpheus."[8] Elizabeth at that date was almost fifty-nine years old.

But if we turn from the court façade of Queen Elizabeth to the robust woman who drank beer and spat and swore " round, mouth-filling oaths ", we have not discovered anything more " real "; for such behaviour was not unique among the great ladies of the time. They were seldom as bloodless as Shakespeare's Olivia. We shall merely have made a sham-antique or " quaint " Elizabeth.

We have to guard against two dangers in particular. We must not react too strongly against the romantic portrait and, by rejecting wholly the courtier's chaste goddess and the poet's fair vestal, run to the opposite extreme. For she *was* romantic. We must not make too much of her brassy, coarse and vulgar side, nor of the red wig and blackened teeth which unflattering foreigners noted in her autumn years. She could be a jade, a scold, a termagant. She was never very beautiful. She was not always brave. She was often hysterical. She could be treacherous and cruel, mean and ungrateful. Without much doubt, she resented her enforced chastity and affected to be more religious than she was. All this is true. But, without possessing the obvious physical charms of some more ordinary women, she was genuinely captivating to many men for many years. She could be gracious, candid, kindly when she chose; and she could display magnanimity, courage, grandeur when they were needed. The romantic portrait flatters and it suppresses much truth but it does not wholly lie.

The other danger to be avoided is that of telescoping time when we think of Queen Elizabeth. The historian must not prolong her youth, as she and her courtiers tried to do; and he must not forget that for half her reign she was, in Ralegh's words, "a lady whom time hath surprised". Nor must we read back into her earlier years the imperious, hook-nosed harridan that she became. We forget that the old lady who could inspire such terror and who was, as a rule, completely self-possessed, had once been the girl of twenty who broke down and cried when her sister sent her to the Tower and who sat upon the steps outside refusing to take shelter from the rain.

Time is all-important in any consideration of her reign. For one thing, hers was the longest reign in English history since that of Edward III, and she died at a greater age than any of her predecessors; and length of days in itself has always been one way into Englishmen's affections. Moreover, we must always distinguish carefully between the three periods into which her reign naturally falls—the hazardous years (up to the coming of Mary Stuart to Carlisle and the rising in the North in 1569) during which the queen was feeling her way and everything was touch and go; the middle years of growing confidence crowned with stupendous victory; and the last fifteen years in which a restive younger generation was growing openly impatient of her ways. No one was ever more aware of time than was Elizabeth herself. She consciously played with it and for it all her life. During her coronation procession she halted before an allegorical figure representing Time : "Time!" she exclaimed, "And Time hath brought me hither." It would ill become historians to be more oblivious of time and to construct a single composite Elizabeth without regard to period.

Time was indeed the essence of Elizabeth's unwritten contract with her subjects; and time was in a very special sense on her side. Time, too, was what England needed more than all else—time for the economic and religious storms to blow themselves out; time for Sir Thomas Gresham and Sir Thomas Smith to reform the currency and restore the national credit; time for Sir William Cecil to mature his forty-year plan for making England self-sufficing and self-reliant; time for a makeshift, political religion to strike roots into the English soil; time for Queen and Parliament to learn one another's frame of mind; time to dispose of rivals for the throne, and to let over-mighty subjects over-reach themselves; time for the new schools to teach the " new men " the New Learning; time for the profiteers to acquire the manners, the culture and the sense of responsibility of educated gentlemen; for the privateers to learn the higher arts of admiralty; for the sonneteers to try their hands at epic or at drama; time to expose the feet of clay in the Spanish colossus, and for the Netherlands to become Spain's running sore; time for the Scots to be detached from France and for France to become torn by civil war; time to grow out of tutelage in diplomacy and in poetry alike, to dispense with the need for a Spanish or a French royal marriage, or with the need to lean on Seneca or Petrarch; time for " the new draperies " (the cloth industry) to be established and for the problem of unemployment to be almost solved; time for commercial travellers to reach the Tsar and the Great Mogul, for the first colonists to arrive at Roanoke Island, for Sir Francis Drake to sail round the world and for Sir John Hawkins to begin the slave trade;* time for the madrigal and the miniature to reach perfection, for the building of Longleat and Hardwick Hall, for the writing of *Arcadia* and *The Faerie Queene*, of *The Ecclesiastical Polity* and *The Advancement of Learning*; time for the youthful " honey-tongued "

* Also for William Adams to reach Japan and to build Japan's first navy.

author of *Venus and Adonis* to conceive a Falstaff and a Hamlet.

On every front it paid Elizabeth's government to play for time, to use delaying tactics, to leave every thorny subject as far as possible alone, to resist all pressure groups, and to avoid almost all decisions. No policy was better adapted to the queen's own temperament, for she had what amounted to a pathological dislike of descending from a fence. She was unbelievably fortunate in being so placed that, in almost every issue that confronted her, any irrevocable decision might well have been more dangerous than indecision. If she married any husband, trouble of one kind or another was certain to ensue. So it was, if she acceded either to the Papists' or to the Puritans' demands. So it was, if she moved too quickly against the old nobility before they committed themselves to armed rebellion. So it was, if she interfered from outside to expedite the Scottish Reformation. So it was, if she let the Netherlands make her or Leicester their sovereign. So it was, if she embarked on open war with Spain before it became inevitable, or if she executed Mary Stuart before Mary made herself no longer tolerable. There was unconscious wisdom even in the ageing Elizabeth's refusal to name her successor, since to have done so would have started a stampede of needy and greedy courtiers to secure the heir-apparent's favour.

Elizabeth learnt very early how to bide her time, and how to hide her feelings; and she learnt also that it might be dangerous to be in any way committed. When she was fifteen she seems to have been not wholly unresponsive to the indecorous, elephantine, buttock-slapping flirtations of the Admiral Seymour who was married to her guardian the Dowager Queen Catherine Parr. Seymour went to the block, and the princess had to live down some scandalous rumours. A heartless priggishness was obviously required of her and she took care to provide it. When she was told of the Admiral's execution she said, " This day died a man with much wit, and very little judgement."

In the reign of her prim and Protestant little brother demureness was the becoming wear. The princess so successfully adopted the right pose that Edward called her " his dear and sweet sister, Temperance ". We also learn that " her maidenly apparel . . . made the noblemen's daughters and wives to be ashamed to be dressed and painted like peacocks ". She even managed to give the impression that she disdained jewellery and fine clothes, and that " she never meddled with money but against her will, but . . . thought to touch it was to defile her pure hands consecrated to turn over good books, to lift up unto God in prayer and to deal alms to the poor ".[4]

The simplicity of her tastes helped her to make friends with what might be called the mammon of righteousness, that is, with the incipient Puritan party. In Mary's reign the princess's modest state and retinue helped to excite sympathy and to make it seem that her sister was treating her in beggarly fashion.[5] This simplicity also saved money. In one year, at the end of Edward's reign, Elizabeth had an income of £6000, audited the accounts herself, and saved £1500—partly by giving no more than £7 15s. 8d. in alms.[6]

She was genuinely frugal; and the first silk stockings she ever wore were given her as a New Year's present in the first year of her reign. She is alleged to have said : " Indeed I like silk stockings well because they are pleasant and fine and delicate and henceforth I shall wear no more cloth stockings."[7]

Perhaps it was in her Puritan phase that she acquired her parsimony. She was later to make a profit from selling munitions to her own soldiers in the year of the Armada. She was to greet Essex on his return from Cadiz with the demand for a strict account of every penny spent. And in 1599 she worked out that the King of France owed her precisely £401,734 16s. 5½d. She could note the poor returns from the sale of Crown lands and say : " My commissioners behave to me as strawberry vendors do to their customers, who lay two or three great strawberries at the mouth of the pottle, and all the rest are little ones; so they give me two or three good prices at the first, and the rest fetch nothing."[8] It may have been partly a certain confidence in her talent for good housekeeping that made her tell her Parliament in 1566, " I thank God I am indued with such qualities that if I were turned out of the realm in my petticoat, I were able to live in any place in Christendom."[9]

She had survived the dangerous times under Mary by lying very low, by covering her tracks, and of course by outwardly conforming to Catholicism. Whether she wrote it or not, the motto scratched on the window-pane at Woodstock represents her policy—

Much suspected by [of] me,
Nothing proved can be.

And she said long afterwards that she had learnt in her sister's reign " how to keep silent ".

When Elizabeth came to the throne she had some lessons still to learn. She was a young woman of twenty-five endowed with body and passions as well as parts. As she said two years later to the Spanish Ambassador, " I wish to confess to you and tell you my secret, which is, that I am no angel." And she went on to say that she had " some affection for Lord Robert ".[10] Lord Robert Dudley, better known as Earl of Leicester, was the son of John Dudley, Duke of Northumberland, and therefore a scion of the best-hated and most obviously parvenu of the new families. Leicester was handsome in a florid way and could cut a dash at court. He knew how to play up to the queen's animal spirits, to the brassy, flamboyant side of her nature. He had little else to commend him, except that he had sold property to supply her wants in Mary's time. Like Elizabeth herself, Leicester had been in mortal danger under Mary, and he might have posed as a Protestant martyr. But he preferred to press his suit to the queen through the good offices of the Spanish ambassador who thought him more malleable than Cecil and a more likely tool for Spain. Leicester was to intrigue with almost every party before he had done. He was unscrupulous and not particularly able. One Spanish ambassador called him "a light and greedy man".[11] Above all, he was a married man; and in September 1560 his wife Amy Robsart was found with a broken neck at the bottom of a staircase, only too soon after it had become known that both he and the queen had openly regretted Amy's existence. After that, any marriage between Elizabeth and Leicester would have been too great a scandal, even in that not over-squeamish age. Leicester might easily have become to Elizabeth the evil genius that Bothwell was to Mary Stuart.

There is little doubt that Elizabeth was in some sense in love with Leicester, though a great deal of doubt as to how far she went with him. She went far enough to worry Cecil; and she shocked the Scottish envoy when she tickled Leicester's neck while publicly investing him with the collar of an earl.[12] Early one morning in August 1565 Leicester took the Spanish ambassador riding in Windsor Park. They returned past the queen's apartments and "Leicester's fool made so much noise calling that she came undressed to the window".[13] Four years earlier the Spanish bishop Quadra thought that the queen and Leicester "went so far" on a barge in the Thames that he took half-seriously Leicester's joking invitation to him to perform the rite of marriage.[14] In 1566 the French ambassador swore to his Spanish colleague that Leicester "had slept with the queen on New Year's night"; but the Spaniard was inclined to attribute this report to the Frenchman's anxiety to smear the queen's reputation and thus prevent her from making any Hapsburg marriage.[15]

It is no more certain whether or not Elizabeth had some sexual disability. We can probably discount the much later tittle-tattle of John Aubrey and Ben Jonson.[16] Yet four different foreign ambassadors thought, independently and early in the reign, that there were "secret reasons" why Elizabeth would not bear children and might not marry at all.[17] Her godson Sir John Harington (inventor of the water-closet), who knew her in private life as well as most men, hints at something similar.[18] Elizabeth may have been speaking the literal truth if she did say to her ladies, as Sir James Melville wrote long afterwards, " The Queen of Scots is lighter of a fair son, while I am but a barren stock ".[19]

On the other hand, later Spanish envoys were willing to give some credence to rumours that the queen had borne Leicester children; and King Philip made serious investigations into the *bona fides* of a young Englishman who claimed to be their son.[20] Perhaps the earlier report of the queen's impotence had been disbelieved, or else lost in the files of the Escorial. In any case it may well have been unfounded. Cecil never seems to have doubted that the queen could and should provide England with an heir; and in 1566 the French ambassador was informed by her doctor that, if she married, he would guarantee ten children.[21]

Whatever the reasons for it, we can confidently believe in her technical innocence. In October 1562 when she believed herself dying of smallpox the queen swore that though she " loved Lord Robert dearly, as God was her witness, nothing improper had ever passed between them."[22] There is something hardly less convincing in the tone of her words to de Silva two years later—" God knows how great a slander it is, and a time will come when the world will know it. My life is in the open, and I have so many witnesses that I cannot understand how so bad a judgement can have been formed of me."[23] We do at least know that, politically, she kept Leicester in his place. " God's death ! My Lord," she once said to him, " I will have here but one mistress and no master "; which, wrote Sir Robert Naunton who reported it, " so quailed my Lord of Leicester, that his feigned humility was, long after, one of his best virtues ".[24]

Her exclamation was in character; for no courtier found that his advice was taken against the queen's or Cecil's better judgment. Even in her flightiest moods she kept court politics and real politics in water-tight compartments.

Her courtiers rose and fell but her ministers, once appointed, stayed till they died in her service. She did take Hatton into favour for his good looks and good dancing, but it took another twenty years before she was sure enough of his more serious gifts to make him Lord Chancellor. And, if she gave Leicester or Essex the command of armies, we must remember that noblemen were trained for warfare, that they had professional advisers, and that high command in war was still (and remained for long afterwards) the prerogative of high rank in society.* The queen also had her courtier-commanders closely overseen. In politics, the courtiers and the nobles held more subordinate positions. Elizabeth did not always *take* advice, but the advice she *listened* to was that of her real ministers, who were far too hard-worked to have time for a courtier's air and graces.

Even so, her ministers must have found her exacting and exasperating. Not only might she box Cecil's ears, or fling her slipper in Walsingham's face,[25] or imprison Davison for executing her warrant for Mary Stuart's death; but, as Harington states, " her wisest men and best councillors were oft sore troubled to know her will in matters of state, so covertly did she pass her judgement ". Besides, he says, she would hold them responsible for anything that went wrong and take the credit for herself when things went well.[26]

Yet the queen had some title to the credit. In the last analysis her policy was more her own than Cecil's. Cecil himself had once (in September 1560) so much distrusted her judgment that he had thought of throwing in his hand and retiring into private life.[27] But Elizabeth acquired more discretion, and Cecil came to know her better and, as he did so, learnt to trust her. Before he died he advised his

* It will be remembered that the Crown Prince of Germany nominally commanded armies in the 1914-18 war. It will also be remembered that some princes—Parma, Gustavus, Condé, Frederick, Eugène—have had real military merits.

son never to press her, once her mind was made up, as she was almost certain to be right.

Cecil was justified : Elizabeth was a very able woman, judged by any standard. She had the usual accomplishments of a Renaissance blue-stocking and could speak six languages, including Latin and Greek, extremely well. Her Italian, for instance, impressed the Venetians as much better than her sister's.[28] She told her Parliament in 1585, " I suppose few that be not professors have read more."[29] She read much history and made, at different times, translations from Xenophon, Tacitus and Sallust as well as from Boethius, Plutarch, Cicero and Horace.[30] She turned to Seneca " when she had been stirred to passion " or " when the soul's quiet was flown away ".[31] She composed some verse and possessed some musical talent. In 1597 when an egregious Polish envoy read her a lecture instead of paying her the usual compliments, she replied impromptu in fluent and vitriolic Latin. She began, " *Expectavi legationem, mihi vere querelam adduxisti* ", told him that he seemed to have read many books but not those which prescribed the manners normally observed between princes, pointed out that his sovereign (being merely an *elected* monarch) could hardly be expected to know better, and ended by turning to her councillors and exclaiming, " God's death ! My Lords, but I have been enforced this day to scour up my old Latin that hath lain long rusting."[32]

Other sovereigns might have competed with her in some at least of these fields. Where she excelled them all was in the astonishing flexibility of her mind, in the quickness of her reactions and in her unfailing intellectual vitality. It is even claimed that she once wrote one letter while dictating another and at the same time listened to " a tale which she made answer unto ".[33] According to Sir John Hayward, when she gave audience " her eye was set upon one, her ear listened to another, her judgement ran upon a third, to a fourth she addressed her speech ; her spirit seemed to be everywhere and yet so entire in her self, as it seemed to be nowhere else ".[34] What is certain is that she could tire out her ministers by consulting them far into the night and yet be ready for government business " before day ".[35] There is some reason to think that she had a Churchillian capacity for sleeping in short snatches and that, at least in her later years, she both slept and ate very little and only irregularly, " at the call of nature ".[36] She had a remarkable memory and reinforced it by taking notes, whereby she would sometimes abash her advisers by confronting them with what they had said " a month before ".[37]

It is also certain that the queen was spring-heeled in the speed of her wit and repartee. She may not have said to a deputation of eighteen tailors, " Good-morning, gentlemen both "* : but she did say, when the French ambassador complained of being kept waiting six days for an answer, " It is true that the world was made in six days, but it was by God, to Whose power the infirmity of man is not to be compared."[38] And when Philip committed a diplomatic incivility by failing to inform her of his wife's death in 1568, she said " she supposed the King of Spain had not wished to write . . . thinking it would not be very seemly that, so soon after the death of the queen his wife, he should be sending letters to a marriageable girl [*une fille à marier*] such as herself ".[39]

Perhaps Elizabeth's ability is best shown in the exploitation of her own personal resources, in the conscious building up of her personal legend. She cut her coat according to her cloth and turned her potential weaknesses into strength. It is true that half the troubles of her reign came from her being a woman ruler; yet she traded on her femininity and used it to rouse the protective instincts of the male. Even the fish-like Philip did not prove wholly insusceptible. Although she claimed to have " the heart and stomach of a king " and although she was rightly described by Robert Cecil as " more than a man and, in truth, sometime less

* " Nine tailors make a man."

than a woman ",[40] her arts were feminine arts and her triumphs were a woman's conquests.

All the scramblings for her favour, all the artificial languishings and flirtations that went on at her court may seem to us, at best, picturesque irrelevancies or, at worst, highly unedifying. But even late in life the queen still had just enough of what can only be called sex-appeal to give a faint tang of reality to the make-believe—which is perhaps its saving grace. Besides, the elaborate *coquetterie* had serious political value, for it kept the courtiers out of real politics. Men who might have had undesirable political ambitions could be side-tracked into seeking court preferment instead. " She ruled," wrote Naunton, " much by factions and parties, which herself both made, upheld and weakened as her own great judgement advised ", playing off the hangers-on of Leicester against those of Norfolk or, later, the Cecilians against the Essexites.[41] The capricious and purely personal basis of her favour helped to break up the factions and to keep them balanced; for favour could be shown to men of every faction, and no one could feel sure of permanent favour or, without impertinence, claim favour as a right.[42] In this way dangerous persons could be kept under the royal eye, and men who might have been disloyal to England could be made devoted to England's queen. She was rightly described long afterwards, in James Harrington's *Oceana*, as " converting her reign through the perpetual love-tricks that passed between her and her people into a kind of romance ".[43]

It is clear that Elizabeth's attractions, at least when she was young, included physical attraction. We may discount much courtiers' flattery, but foreign observers have some right to be believed. A Venetian in 1557 thought the princess had a countenance more " gratiosa " than " bella ". " But," he wrote, " she is tall and well-formed with a good complexion although sallow [olivastra]; she has fine eyes and above all a beautiful hand of which she makes a display."[44] Another in 1554 had thought her " bella " and added that " such an air of dignified majesty pervades all her actions that no one can fail to suppose she is a queen ".[45] The Scotsman Melville noted in 1564 that her hair was " more reddish than yellow " and that " in appearance " it " curled naturally ".[46] Sir John Hayward, writing after Elizabeth was dead, described her as " of stature mean*, slender, straight and amiably composed; of such state in her carriage, as every motion of her seemed to bear majesty : her hair was inclined to pale yellow, her forehead large and fair; . . . her eyes lively and sweet, but short-sighted; her nose somewhat rising in the midst; the whole compass of her countenance somewhat long but yet of admirable beauty, not so much in that which is termed the flower of youth, as in a most delightful composition of majesty and modesty ".[47]

Naunton called her " tall, of hair and complexion fair, and therewith well-favoured, but high-nosed, of limbs and feature neat; and . . . of stately and majestic deportment ". He also thought her more like her father than her mother, although " the atrocity of her father's nature " was " rebated in hers by the mother's sweeter inclinations ".[48] In this connection there is the strange story of William Parry, the half-mad Welsh spy and traitor, who " had vowed to kill her, being alone with her in the garden at Richmond and then resolved to act that tragedy, was so daunted with the majesty of her presence, in which he then saw the image of her grandfather King Henry VII . . . that his heart would not suffer his hand to execute that which he had resolved ".†[49]

Even in old age Elizabeth still had vivaciousness and a certain charm as well as an imposing presence, though we need not believe the German visitor who saw her in 1592

* i.e. medium.

† In his confession, as recorded in the *State Trials*, Parry says that she looked like her father; and, in any case, Parry (executed in 1585) is unlikely to have seen Henry VII in the flesh. But John Clapham, who tells the story, repeats elsewhere that Elizabeth was known to resemble her grandfather.

(when she was fifty-nine) and thought " she need not . . . yield much to a girl of sixteen "[50]; nor yet another German, Thomas Platter, who found her in 1599 "very youthful still in appearance, seeming no more than twenty years of age ".[51]

Paul Hentzner's account, written in 1598, has a truer ring. "Next came the Queen, . . . very majestic; her face oblong, fair but wrinkled; her eyes small, yet black and pleasant; her nose a little hooked, her lips narrow and her teeth black (a defect the English seem subject to, from their too great use of sugar); she had in her ears two pearls with very rich drops; her hair was of an auburn colour but false; upon her head she had a small crown; her bosom was uncovered as all the English ladies have it till they marry. . . . Her hands were slender, her fingers rather long, and her stature neither tall nor low; her air was stately, and her manner of speaking mild and obliging."[52] De Maisse, the French ambassador who saw her in 1597, got a very similar impression but was a little more malicious, indicating that the queen's dress was very fantastic, not to say indecent; that the uncovered bosom was " somewhat wrinkled "; that she kept pulling open her dress " so that one saw the whole of her stomach "; that the pearls were " of no great worth "; that the gaps in her teeth made it hard to understand what she said; that she wore " a great reddish-coloured wig "; and that " so far as may be she keeps her dignity ".[53] Some of the Venetians were equally frank; and one of them reports that in 1580 Alençon had become less ardent in his wooing when " he called to mind the advanced age and repulsive physical nature of the queen [le brutte qualita del corpo della Regina] ".[54] But one Venetian speaks, even in 1603, of her " past but never quite lost beauty ".[55]

Elizabeth was sensitive enough about her fading charms, refusing (it is said) to have a mirror in her palaces, making embarrassing jokes about her ugliness and " fishing " for denials of it,[56] forbidding any reference to the succession, and saying pathetically to her godson, " When thou dost feel creeping time at thy gate, these fooleries will please thee less."[57]

Nevertheless her immense vitality triumphed over all bodily ailments and decay. She was never physically robust and nearly died of smallpox in 1562. There is some evidence that in her late teens she was quite seriously ill, mainly with a form of dropsy. In middle life she had an ulcer on her leg which did not heal for eight or nine years. She nearly fainted from the weight of her clothes while making one of her great speeches in Parliament. In middle and old age she suffered from headaches, from nerve-storms that suggest hysteria, and from chronic melancholia. She was claustrophobic, abhorred shut windows and complained of suffocation if people crowded round her. Once on her way to chapel " she was suddenly overcome with a shock of fear" and had to return to her apartment.[58] She had a peculiar horror of certain smells, especially of the scented leather so fashionable in her day. This she used once as an excuse for refusing a favour to Sir Roger Williams (the original of Fluellen) who was wearing a new and smelly pair of boots, although tradition says he got the better of her by saying, " Tut, tut, Madame, 'tis my suit that stinks ".[59]

In view of her delicacy, it is remarkable that even late in life she chose to travel on horseback rather than by coach, although a horse may well have been better sprung than a Tudor coach on Tudor roads. It is not less remarkable, even if unedifying, that at the age of sixty-six, in the words of an Italian observer, " on the day of the Epiphany the Queen held a great feast, in which the head of the Church of England and Ireland was to be seen in her old age dancing three or four gaillards ".[60] Her style of dancing, at any rate when she was young, involved some leaping from the ground, as a picture at Penshurst suggests and as James Melville implied when he told her that the Queen of Scots " danced not so high and disposedly as she did ".[61]

She was tougher in mind and spirit even than in body.

Although she had nervous moments, courage invariably supervened. Sir John Perrot, her deputy in Ireland (who may have been her bastard half-brother), is reported to have said once, " Lo now she is ready to be-piss herself for fear of the Spaniards "[62]; yet he could also write in 1586, " I am glad to hear that, notwithstanding all her troubles, she carrieth an invincible mind that showeth from whom she came ".[63] Perhaps she was like her grandfather Henry VII, of whom it was said : " In times of danger there was no man more confident than he, and out of danger, less secure."[64]

Even the Spanish bishop Quadra had to admit that the young queen " made a brave show and bore herself gallantly " while she was exercising, mounted on her Neapolitan jennet, with the London train bands when war with France and Scotland was expected in 1560.[65] When she heard of Rizzio's murder, she told the Spanish ambassador that if she had been in Mary Stuart's place she " would have taken her husband's dagger and stabbed him with it ", though she hastened to add that she would not do this to the Archduke Charles if he became her husband.[66] When another Spanish envoy, Mendoza, told her in 1581 that if she would not listen to his words, " it would be necessary to see whether cannons would not make her hear them better ", she replied at once, " without any passion but as one would repeat the words of a farce, speaking very low ", that if he used threats she would put him " into a place where he could not say a word ".[67]

All her adult life Elizabeth lived in danger of a violent death; and she knew it, though she took little notice of it. She slept at one time with a naked sword by her bedside but she rejected her ministers' advice to avoid public appearances. Once one of her bargemen was wounded in the arm by a gun fired from the shore, but she did not turn a hair. She gave the man her own handkerchief to staunch the wound, saying " Be of good cheer, for you will never want. For the bullet was meant for me."

There is something unmistakably convincing about the queen's great speech to the soldiers at Tilbury when the Armada was coming up the Channel—" My loving people : we have been persuaded by some that are careful of our safety to take heed how we commit ourselves to armed multitudes, for fear of treachery; but I assure you, I do not desire to live to distrust my faithful, loving people. Let tyrants fear. . . . I am come among you, as you see, at this time, not for my recreation and disport, but being resolved, in the midst and heat of the battle, to live and die amongst you all. . . . I know that I have the body of a weak and feeble woman, but I have the heart and stomach of a king, and of a King of England, too; and I think foul scorn that Parma, or Spain, or any prince of Europe should dare to invade the borders of my realm; to which rather than any dishonour should grow by me, I will myself take up arms, I myself will be your general, judge and rewarder of every one of your virtues in the field.''[68] Even twelve years after the Armada she insisted on going on with her dinner when she was told that Essex was raising armed rebellion in the City streets; but after dinner she could hardly be restrained from going in person to see if a single rebel would in fact dare to face her. Elizabeth was sixty-seven years old at the time.

The rebels might well have quailed, for the queen could be very formidable. Even her own councillors had their bad moments. When they decided, in the absence of Cecil and herself, in 1569, that the succession question ought to be settled by marrying Mary Stuart to the Duke of Norfolk, they all declined to tell Elizabeth of their decision; and when Norfolk himself tried to tell her, " he fell into an ague and was fain to get him to bed without his dinner ''.[69] According to Fuller " she had a piercing eye, wherewith she used to touch what metal strangers were made of who came into her presence ", and " counted it a pleasant conquest with her majestic look to dash strangers out of countenance ".[70]

Elizabeth certainly had her hard, cruel side. It is true that she tore up some evidence given to her about those who had worked against her in her sister's reign.[71] It is true that Elizabeth had innumerable *crises de nerfs* before she could bring herself to execute Norfolk or the Queen of Scots or Essex. But she was always jumpy before making irrevocable decisions and always anxious to avoid personal responsibility for them. She was quite willing that Paulet, Mary Stuart's jailor, should execute Mary on his own initiative without a warrant; and when he refused, Elizabeth complained of his " daintiness and perjury " and of " the niceness of these precise fellows ".[72] Nor had she the same hesitation about the deaths of humbler folk. She hounded Sussex on when he was pacifying the North after the rebellion of 1569, and ordered hangings in every village green and market place where the rebels had assembled—" the bodies . . . to remain till they fall to pieces where they hang ".[73]

No wonder Harington records that in her wrath the queen " left no doubtings whose daughter she was ".[74] No wonder that when he saw her, during the Essex crisis, " stamping with her feet at ill news and thrusting her rusty sword at times into the arras in great rage ", he fled from court and vowed to stay in his " poor castle of Kelston . . . I will eat Aldbourne rabbits, and get fish . . . from the man at Curry-Rival; and get partridge and hares when I can, and my venison where I can; and leave all great matters to those that like them better than myself ".[75] And yet he says also that " when she smiled, it was a pure sunshine ", and that " her mind was oft time like the gentle air that cometh from the westerly point in a summer's morn ".[76]

The queen could indeed be genuinely kind. She insisted on Burghley's being seated in her presence in his gouty old age and fed him with her own hand during his last illness; and she could write touching condolence letters to friends who had lost sons in her wars. " Mine own Crow ", she wrote with her own hand to Lady Norris, " Now that

Nature's common work is done, and he that was born to die hath paid his tribute, let that Christian discretion stay the flux of your immoderate grieving, which hath instructed you . . . that nothing of this kind hath happened but by God's Divine Providence. . . . More at this time we will not write of this unsilent subject ".[77]

Elizabeth could salt her mercy and her kindness with a touch of wit, as on the occasion when she pardoned her one-time jailor Sir Henry Bedingfield, and told him, " if we have any prisoner whom we would have sharply and straitly kept, we will send for you ". But occasionally parsimony or malice could put a sting into apparent generosity, as it did when the Queen of Scots arrived in England, having fled her kingdom so hurriedly as to have no change of clothes. Elizabeth offered to supply her wants and sent a parcel by Sir Francis Knollys which, to his embarrassment, was found to contain " two torn shifts, two pieces of black velvet, two pairs of shoes and nothing else ". Knollys was reduced to saying " that her Highness's maid had mistaken and sent such things necessary for such a maid-servant as she was herself ".[78]

Elizabeth's attitude to the Queen of Scots was unavoidably ambivalent. She may have had a natural feminine envy of Mary's fatal charm for men. She knew that Mary was her legal heiress; and Elizabeth had a morbid horror of contemplating a successor—all talk of it she looked on as seeing her own winding-sheet. Besides she had herself been, during her sister's reign, in the same position, and she must have known what it involved. She had good cause to know how the factious and the malcontent will manoeuvre to secure a residuary interest with the heir presumptive. She knew that Mary was the constant focus for rebellion and assassination plots, and a constant temptation to potential invaders. Mary was Spenser's false Duessa and she appears in Elizabeth's own verse as " the daughter of debate that eke discord doth sow ". Almost certainly Elizabeth believed Mary guilty of killing Darnley and also guilty of conspiring with English traitors. Yet to kill Mary might precipitate the rebellion or invasion which everybody feared. To kill Mary was also foreign to Elizabeth's accustomed clemency and to her native fear of drastic action. All the same, it is remarkable that Mary survived for almost nineteen years after becoming Elizabeth's prisoner. Henry VII and Henry VIII had a way of eliminating dangerous relatives with less delay —and of making fewer bones about it.

Mary's existence not only encouraged the feudal, Catholic, conservative opposition to Elizabeth; it tried the patience of her most loyal subjects, the would-be Protestant crusaders. It was an ever-present reminder of Elizabeth's paltering and procrastination, of her seeming want of nerve. Besides, it must have been largely because she could not bear to contemplate Mary's succeeding to her throne, that Elizabeth was at least half serious when she sought the hand of foreign princes. She may have meant it when she told her first Parliament that she intended to live and die a virgin[79]; and it may have been, in part, Mary's subsequent behaviour which made Elizabeth think of changing her mind. The marriage projects tried the patience of good Protestants still further—especially the Alençon project. Spenser satirised it in *Mother Hubberd's Tale* and Sidney addressed to the queen herself a very frank and most courageous protest.[80] It was for writing a pamphlet against the Alençon marriage that the Puritan Stubbes had his right hand cut off; but such was his loyalty that he took off his hat with his left hand and cried " God Save the Queen !" before he fainted.

Elizabeth had constantly to offend her most ardent supporters; and she was safe enough in doing so. There was no one for whom they could desert her, whereas there were claimants for the allegiance of her conservative or luke-warm subjects. It was therefore obviously more dangerous to offend the less loyal; and of course there was always the danger of provoking foreign powers prematurely. It was these considerations which very largely governed the queen's religious policy. She was committed to the breach with Rome by her very birth and could not heal the breach without declaring herself a bastard. She had been brought up by Protestant tutors; and foreign ambassadors found her strangely ignorant of Catholic doctrine. She had been in danger under Mary partly because her religious views were suspect; and Elizabeth was morally committed to doing something for those who had prayed and plotted and suffered for her. In any case, there could be no going back on the dissolution of the monasteries and no renewal of the fires of Smithfield. Besides, the Protestants were not only her most loyal subjects but included the most vigorous of the men of substance and the ablest and most learned of the available divines. She gave them what they wanted most, a Protestant theology. The Catholic or near-Catholic majority were less interested in the higher theological flights. For most of such men religion meant what they saw going on in the chancel of their parish church on Sunday morning. To keep them undisturbed the queen therefore retained many "rags of popery" in liturgy and in vestments. There was no *via media*, unless two extremes—a Protestant extreme in doctrine and a Catholic extreme in ritual—can be said to cancel out and form a compromise.

The extremists of both parties were temporarily hoodwinked. But as time went on the Protestant extremists became increasingly impatient of concessions to "superstition" which seemed to be dictated by mere reason of state. Many of their leaders had become bishops but proved themselves unable or unwilling to go further than the queen permitted—hence the growing agitation against bishops as such. The Catholics, discredited after Mary's reign and lacking good leaders for a time, gave little trouble until the arrival of the Queen of Scots precipitated a new crisis. After the Rising in the North and the Papal Excommunication of Elizabeth, divided loyalties and agonies of conscience were forced upon her Catholic subjects. Elizabeth eventually took to violence. Between two and three hundred men were hanged or disembowelled, and others died in prison. Nominally at least, they died for political offences; although to make any hard and fast distinction between heresy and treason in the sixteenth century would be anachronistic. In times when religion was taken so seriously, how could men who had a different religion from their ruler's be thought of as reliable subjects? In any case, it was not easy to be wholly tolerant of men who would not have been tolerant themselves had they been in power.

Elizabeth burnt precisely four men for heresy, all of them Anabaptists who would have suffered under any other government in Christendom. During her forty-five years the victims of Elizabeth's persecution amounted to no more than the number burnt by Mary in less than three years. Besides, Elizabeth had an excuse which Mary could scarcely plead. For more than half of Elizabeth's reign the country was fighting for survival in a war that was real enough long before it was formally declared. England could not afford to tolerate active sympathisers with a hostile power; and Elizabeth was at least justified by one result—her kingdom escaped religious civil war.

The queen asked for no more than outward uniformity and she refused to " make windows into men's souls ". She was in a sense quite cynical. At least she had no patience with those who wanted to persecute or go to war over the *minutiae* of theological dogma, or with those who " made too many subtle scannings " of God's will. " There is only one Jesus Christ ", she is reputed to have said, " and all the rest is a dispute over trifles "; and she asked the King of Spain why it mattered to him if his Dutch subjects chose to go to the Devil in their own way. She also told his ambassador that she hoped to be saved as well as the Bishop of Rome.[81]

Whether for diplomatic or for aesthetic reasons, Elizabeth preserved some Catholic ornaments in her private chapel; and she gave several indications of believing in some sort of Real Presence in the Eucharist. She was certainly shocked by the irreverent treatment of the Sacrament in a masque played by Cambridge undergraduates in 1564; when one entered " in the figure of a dog with the Host in his mouth ", the queen flounced out of the hall " using strong language ".[82] This is not inconsistent with the Lutheranism in which she had been brought up. It is probably untrue that she had no genuine beliefs. Her prayers do not always read like academic exercises. It does seem that she at least believed in a special Providence that watched over her and England. Her eloquence was most convincing when she said such things as " I think that, at the worst, God has not yet decided that England shall cease to stand where she does, or at least that God has not given the power to overthrow her to those men who would like to undertake it ".[83]

Of course the queen was Erastian in ecclesiastical matters, and she showed a certain disrespect for her own clergy. She valued bishops only as a means of keeping the Church under her own control; and she was quite capable of keeping a bishop's see vacant to augment her revenue. She made the Bishop of Ely give up his London property to Sir Christopher Hatton—it is still called Hatton Garden. And when the bishop proved recalcitrant, she got a courtier to remind him that " she is right King Henry, her father, if any strive with her " and to threaten that enquiries might be made into the amount of illicit enclosure the bishop was making in his diocese and the amount of lead and brick he was selling from his neglected houses.[84] She could tell a bishop or a dean to change the subject if he touched in his sermon upon unwelcome matters such as " the vanity of decking the body too finely ".[85] She rather frowned on any preaching, as being a cause of disputatiousness; and one of her reasons for disliking the Puritans was their insistence on " a preaching ministry ". She feared, too, that the Presbyterian system would weaken her grip on the national Church. That her objection was scarcely conscientious can be proved by her letting Presbyterianism become the established religion of the Channel Islands.

The Puritans were, naturally, the war party, anxious to join hands across the sea with a Protestant " International " and to defy the three corners of the Catholic world. They saw the queen as a drag on the wheel, as a wet blanket damping down their ardour. The Puritans were not only the forward party; theirs was the religion of a self-appointed spiritual aristocracy, despising as " superstitious " the artificial aids to worship required by weaker brethren. Among the Puritans were to be found most of the " intellectuals " and many of the " romantics "; and we ought not to be surprised at finding Sidney and Spenser in their ranks. Puritan rigour and Puritan energy braced and inspired many Elizabethan men of action; and, again, we ought not to be surprised to learn that the watchword and the countersign in Martin Frobisher's fleet were two theological propositions—" Before the World was God " and " After God came Christ His Son ".[86] Belief in themselves as an Elect helped to breed the English adventurers' self-confidence, and it passed easily into a belief that the English were God's chosen people, as we may see from the words of John Davis the explorer : " There is no doubt but that we of England are this saved people, by the eternal and infallible presence of the Lord predestinated to be sent unto these Gentiles in the sea. . . . For are not we only set upon Mount Zion to give light to all the rest of the world? Have not we the true handmaid of the Lord to rule us, unto whom the eternal majesty of God hath revealed His truth and supreme power of excellency?"[87]

The adventurers were inclined to attribute the queen's caution to want of trust in the Almighty, or even to want of patriotism. We cannot blame them for not having learnt from later historians to speak of Elizabeth's " masterly inactivity ".

On the eve of the Cadiz expedition of 1596 the impetuous Essex wrote that " the queen wrangles with our action for no cause but because it is in hand. . . . I know I shall never do her service but against her will ".[88] But in the real emergency the queen was not irresolute, and her caution was sometimes due to her clear head and her sense of reality. There were times when she saw difficulties and felt responsibilities of which the hotheads were unaware.

Above all, Elizabeth was not unpatriotic and she was not afraid. In 1593 she told her Parliament, with reference to the King of Spain, " I fear not all his threatenings. His great preparations and mighty forces do not stir me. For though he come against me with a greater power than ever was his Invincible Navy, I doubt not but (God assisting me, upon Whom I always trust) I shall be able to defeat him and overthrow him. For my cause is just. I heard say, when he attempted his last invasion, some upon the sea-coasts forsook their towns and fled up higher into the country and left all naked and exposed to his entrance. But I swear unto you, by God, if I knew those persons . . . I will make them know and feel what it is to be fearful in so urgent a cause."[89]

It is true that she did vacillate, that she was a nervous passenger who was apt to snatch at the wheel whatever course was taken. But this was partly because she herself knew a good deal about driving. There were, too, occasions when Elizabeth took risks which her advisers would not have taken, and occasions when she sailed nearer the wind than they would have dared. She often called the bluff of rebels or of foreign powers when others had not seen that it had been a bluff. It is not surprising that in the end she drove Philip, who was described as " a king who has never shown any passion in good or evil fortune ", to seize a candelabra and vow that " he would pawn even that to be avenged on the Queen ".[90]

All the same, Elizabeth could be ultra-cautious, and some of her vacillation was deep-seated and perhaps neurotic. There was some truth in what the carrier said when he had called three times to fetch her baggage from Windsor and each time was told that the queen had changed her mind about leaving—" Now I see that the queen is a woman as well as my wife ". The queen overheard him from a window and exclaimed, "What a villain is this!" but "sent him three angels to stop his mouth".[91]

Elizabeth was indeed a woman, and a woman thwarted of a woman's normal satisfactions. Some of her weaknesses may have been the result. The caprices, the jealousies, the tantrums, the nerve-storms, the fits of depression which made her a burden to herself and to others, may have been in part the revenge of outraged nature. It may be significant that the queen broke down and wept real tears in front of four of her Councillors when she realised that her last chance of marriage had disappeared.[92] Yet consciously or unconsciously she may well have known that, though she might often finger marriage proposals as diplomatic cards, nothing concrete was likely to come of them. She was, almost from her accession, "the imperial votaress"; and a votaress is a devotee who has made renunciations, a chosen victim who suffers that the multitude may live.

Her devotion condemned her to a loneliness which she felt increasingly as more and more of her old friends predeceased her. There is pathos in the queen's attempts in old age to find a new Leicester and to suck vitality from Essex and from others of the young. She was condemned, as perhaps all monarchs are in some degree, to a life of artificiality. "We princes," she said, "are set as it were upon stages in the sight and view of all the world."[93] For this reason she had to pose and posture, she had to be the consummate actress that she was. It was essential that her marriage projects should at least seem to be in earnest; and it was essential to deceive foreign governments and on occasion even her own advisers, as to her real intentions.

Perhaps the one unmistakably genuine emotion she had, the one which was least a pose, was her sense of England, her sense of obligation to her people. Her eloquence, always remarkable, beat highest in her last, her "golden" speech —"and though God hath raised me high, yet this I count the glory of my reign; that I have reigned with your loves".[94]

T.   F

Elizabeth was a patriot but not a jingo; for she was also, in a sense, a pacifist—perhaps the best kind of patriot. It was not only because peace was exceedingly necessary to heal the wounds and foster the resources of the distracted, bankrupt and humiliated England she inherited. It was not only because peace was so much cheaper than war. It was not only that war involved action and decision. The queen really loved peace for its own sake. She was always offering her services as a mediator in the religious and political strife of foreign states—and not always with an eye to getting something out of it. Elizabeth might have become Queen of the Netherlands. She might, once English naval supremacy had become so clear, have tried to found an English empire overseas or to make the Spanish Main an English Main. But she did not. Instead she told her Parliament in 1593 : " It might be thought simplicity in me that all this time of my reign I have not sought to advance my territories and enlarge my dominions; for opportunity hath served me to do it. . . . But . . . my mind was never to invade my neighbours, or to usurp over any. I am contented to reign over mine own, and to rule as a just prince ".[95]

On the home front the queen's caution, and her pacifism, took the form of letting certain not over-wakeful dogs lie. As a result, she let major problems pass unsolved to her successor. Since she could, as a rule, just make ends meet, she made no effort to put the Crown on a permanently solvent basis. Since the House of Commons, though it was clearly developing muscles of its own, could in the last resort be made to kiss her hand, she evaded the problem of defining its constitutional position and rights. Since the Puritans, however clamorous their demands for more godly and more thorough reformation, remained in fact the most fanatically loyal of all her subjects as well as the most vigorous and enterprising, she avoided any final reckoning with them about the character of the national church.

Above all, Elizabeth let the undeclared war between the

old aristocracy and the new remain undecided. She drew her principal advisers mainly from the "new men" but she always retained a face-saving quorum of feudal magnates on her Council. And she showed herself most reluctant to create new peers, even when the passing of a government bill by the House of Lords seemed doubtful. She also rebuked Sir Philip Sidney for his effrontery, as a mere knight, in challenging the Earl of Oxford to a duel; and she rated Essex for cheapening knighthood by conferring it on so many of his officers who were too poor to count as gentlemen. Socially and politically, Elizabeth was a conservative, preferring the older, more clearly graded, hierarchic social structure to the more fluid, more patently plutocratic society that was coming to be. The queen liked "degree, priority and place", and she liked them to be based on ancient and on landed riches.

Elizabeth may have had her reasons for thinking the new men somewhat crude. Even Burghley could be a trifle shameless on the necessity of social climbing. He wrote some maxims for the guidance of Robert Cecil which read exactly like the advice of a self-made merchant to his son. "Use great providence and circumspection in choosing thy wife. . . . It is an action of life, like unto a stratagem of war, wherein a man can err but once. . . . Let her not be poor how generous soever. For a man can buy nothing in the market with gentility." One of Burghley's few mistakes had been to marry for love when he was very young; his first wife was poor but she died young, and when he remarried the mistake was not repeated. "Marry thy daughters in time lest they marry themselves. . . . Undertake no suit against a poor man", because in doing so "thou makest him thy compeer. . . . If thou hast cause to bestow any great gratuity let it be something which may be daily in sight. Otherwise, in this ambitious age, thou shalt remain like a hop without a pole." "Neither borrow money of a neighbour or a friend, but of a stranger, where paying for it thou shalt hear no more of it." "Let thy hospitality be modest . . . rather plentiful than sparing but not costly."[96] Perhaps there is good ground for the tradition that Polonius is Burghley. Robert Cecil made an apt pupil. He was one day to instruct his own wife " not to let anybody know that she paid under 3s. 10d. a yard for her cloth of silver. I marvel she is so simple as to tell anybody what she pays for everything ".[97]

Nor did the new men play their political games in a particularly gentlemanly fashion. There is some reason to think that Burghley " planted " the traitor Doughty on Drake's ship, to sabotage the expedition and so prevent an imbroglio with Spain. Walsingham was relatively upright and puritanical; at least he made no money in the queen's service. Yet such was his thirst for knowledge that he used his spies to tap the queen's own correspondence with Burghley. Robert Cecil secretly corresponded with the King of Scots long before Elizabeth was dead; and later he took a pension from the King of Spain. It would be understandable if Elizabeth sometimes preferred the manners and morals of less efficient and more old-fashioned gentlemen.

Certainly Elizabeth was determined that any deluge should take place after her. Perhaps her long experience suggested to her that if she delayed long enough, most problems would solve themselves, as indeed so many of her problems had done. Waiting for time to do its work had long become second nature to her. All her life she had been waiting or, as it were, listening for something. This was not due merely to constitutional indecision or to deliberate opportunism; nor was it merely a feeling that if only she could hold on long enough, the situation might grow better and could hardly grow worse. It was connected with her belief in the Providence that watched over England or, more precisely, with her belief in England. She was waiting " to distinguish the voice of her people from the clamour of a faction "—the advice given in a later century to " The Patriot King ". She was waiting to see what England as a whole was really going to want, waiting for England to become self-conscious and self-confident. She would not give in to Catholics or Puritans because she knew that, given time, a new English religion would grow up from the native soil. She would not marry to make political alliances because she thought it better for England to win her own battles without allies. She refused help because she knew that eventually England would save herself. It was like Edward III letting the Black Prince win his spurs.

Even on the queen's death-bed a grim patience was mingled with her wonted defiance and self-containment. Elizabeth, though obviously very ill, refused to go to bed but sat for days " low upon her cushions " to wait for her death. " All about her ", says her kinsman Robert Carey, " could not persuade her either to take any sustenance, or to go to bed." She was melancholic and sat or lay inter-minably, at times semi-conscious, " with her finger in her mouth "; but in a lucid moment she insisted " that she knew of nothing in this world worthy of troubling her ". And when Robert Cecil told her that she *must* go to bed, she said, " The word ' must ' is not to be used to princes. . . . Little man, little man. . . . Ye know that I must die, and that makes ye so presumptuous."[98]

There can be no docketing or summarising of Queen Elizabeth. As a near-contemporary wrote, " For her own mind, what that really was I must leave, as a thing doubly inscrutable, both as she was a woman and a queen."[99] But clearly she had something nearer genius than any earlier or later occupant of her throne. In the year of the Armada the Pope himself said " She is a great woman; and were she only Catholic she would be without her match."[100] Certainly, among all English sovereigns, no others—not even her own father—have impressed themselves so indelibly upon the popular memory and imagination. It was not for nothing that November 17th, the date of her accession, was a national holiday for two hundred years. Nor is it a wonder that in 1589 a forgotten Westminster schoolboy called John Slye, whose dog-eared text of Caesar has been discovered in an Oxford library, should have scribbled in the margins some doggerel that would be a little odd from a schoolboy in any other period.

> The rose is red, the leaves are green.
> God save Elizabeth, our noble Queen.

He scribbled profusely all over the book, but what occurs most often is the single word " Elizabeth ".[101]

A SELECT BIBLIOGRAPHY

The books listed here are intended for the guidance of the "general reader" interested in pursuing Tudor history further. No attempt has been made to achieve the kind of completeness a research worker might require. Much of the contemporary material appears in my own references. Many of the books listed below contain detailed bibliographies. I have omitted numerous well-known older books which have become seriously "dated".

The best short introductions to Tudor history are Conyers Read, *The Tudors: Personalities and Politics in Sixteenth Century England* (1936) and S. T. Bindoff, *Tudor England* (1950).

The best fuller narrative history of the period is now G. R. Elton, *England under the Tudors* (1955) but H. A. L. Fisher's and A. F. Pollard's volumes in *The Political History of England* (1906 and 1910), J. D. Mackie, *The Earlier Tudors* (1952) and J. B. Black, *The Reign of Elizabeth* (1936) should also be consulted. The classical Victorian works by J. A. Froude, *A History of England from the Fall of Wolsey to the Defeat of the Armada* (12 vols. 1856-70) and R. W. Dixon, *A History of the Church of England from the Abolition of the Roman Jurisdiction* (6 vols. 1878-1902) are full, readable and by no means wholly discredited.

The best biographies of Henry VII are by G. Temperley (1917) and C. Williams (1937), the former fully documented, the latter imaginative and stimulating. J. Gairdner's (1902) is small but sound.

For Henry VIII A. F. Pollard's biography (1902), long the standard work, has been superseded by J. J. Scarisbrick's (1968). See also J. J. Bagley *Henry VIII and his Times* (1962), L. B. Smith *Henry VIII, The Mask of Royalty* (1967) and *The Letters of King Henry VIII* ed. M. St.Clair Byrne (1936).

For Edward VI nothing is better than the biographical introduction by J. G. Nichols to *The Literary Remains of Edward VI* (2 vols. 1857). H. Chapman, *The Last Tudor King* (1958) is full, readable and interesting although imperfectly documented. Edward's diary and other works have been well edited by W. K. Jordan (1966) who has also written *Edward VI, The Young King* (1968) and *Edward VI, The Threshold of Power* (1970).

The two outstanding lives of Mary Tudor, both fully documented, are by B. White (1935) and H. F. M. Prescott (1940). See also H. Simpson, *The Spanish Marriage* (1933) and H. Clifford's *Life of Jane Dormer, Duchess of Feria,* ed. J. Stevenson (1887).

Of the numerous modern biographies of Elizabeth none are documented except B. W. Beckingsale, *Elizabeth I* (1963), an admirable monograph. Among older works much the best are those by M. Creighton (1899) and Sir J. E. Neale (1934), although neither is documented. A short but good recent work is J. Hurstfield, *Elizabeth I and the Unity of England* (1960). See also M. Waldman, *Elizabeth and Leicester* (1944); *The Letters of Queen Elizabeth* ed. G. B. Harrison (1935); J. Nichols, *The Progresses and Public Processions of Queen Elizabeth* (3 vols. 1823); *The Public Speaking of Queen Elizabeth* ed. G. P. Rice (1951). A good recent biography is N. Williams, *Elizabeth I, Queen of England* (1967). R. C. Strong, *Portraits of Elizabeth I* (1963) is authoritative on the Queen's iconography.

For other biographies of the period, see vol. II of *Who's Who in History* by C. R. N. Routh (1964); also various essays in *The Great Tudors*, ed. K. Garvin (1935). Other royal biographies include G. Mattingly, *Catherine of Aragon* (1942); P. Friedman, *Anne Boleyn* (2 vols. 1884); L. Baldwin Smith, *A Tudor Tragedy* [Catherine Howard] (1961); H. Chapman, *Lady Jane Grey* (1962) and T. F. Henderson, *Mary Queen of Scots* (1905).

Among numerous other biographies the best are possibly R. W. Chambers, *Thomas More* (1935); A. F. Pollard,

Wolsey (1929); A. G. Dickens, *Thomas Cromwell and the English Reformation* (1959); S. E. Lehmberg, *Sir Thomas Elyot, Tudor Humanist* (1960); J. Ridley, *Thomas Cranmer* (1962); J. F. Mozley, *William Tyndale* (1937); *John Foxe and his Book* (1940) and *Coverdale and his Bibles* (1953); J. A. Muller, *Stephen Gardiner and the Tudor Reaction* (1926); W. Schenk, *Reginald Pole, Cardinal of England* (1950); M. Dewar, *Sir Thomas Smith, a Tudor Intellectual in Office* (1964); Conyers Read, *Mr Secretary Walsingham* (3 vols. 1925), *Mr Secretary Cecil and Queen Elizabeth* (1955) and *Lord Burghley and Queen Elizabeth* (1960); G. B. Harrison, *Life and Death of Robert Devereux, Earl of Essex* (1937); V. J. K. Brook, *Whitgift and the English Church* (1957); also *A Life of Archbishop Parker* (1962); J. Buxton, *Sir Philip Sidney and the English Renaissance* (1954); D. B. Quinn, *Ralegh and the British Empire* (1947); A. L. Rowse, *Sir Richard Grenville* (1937).

Essays of general interest for the Tudor period can be found in *Shakespeare's England* ed. C. T. Onions (2 vols. 1916); *Life under the Tudors* ed. J. Morpurgo and O. Morris (1950); Sir J. E. Neale, *Essays in Tudor History* (1958) and J. H. Hexter, *Reappraisals in History* (1961). Among important books of general interest are A. L. Rowse, *The England of Elizabeth: the Structure of Society* (1951); G. Mattingly, *Renaissance Diplomacy* (1955); A. H. Dodd, *Life in Elizabethan England* (1961); P. Williams *Life in Tudor England* (1969); and L. Stone, *The Crisis of the Aristocracy (1558-1641)* (1965).

For political and constitutional matters see G. R. Elton, *The Tudor Constitution*, (1960), *The Tudor Revolution in Government* (1953); K. W. M. Pickthorn. *Early Tudor Government* (2 vols. 1934); W. S. Holdsworth, *A History of English Law*, vol. IV (1924); W. G. Zeeveld, *Foundations of Tudor Policy* (1948); J. Hurstfield, *The Queen's Wards* (1958); Sir J. E. Neale, *The Elizabethan House of Commons* (1949) and *Elizabeth I and her Parliaments* (2 vols. 1953 and 1957); also *Elizabethan Government and Society* ed. S. T. Bindoff, J. Hurstfield and C. H. Williams (1961). W. MacCaffrey, *The Shaping of the Elizabethan Régime* (1969); S. E. Lehmberg, *The Reformation Parliament* (1970); R. B. Wernham, *Before the Armada: the growth of English foreign policy, 1485-1588* (1966).

For economic and social history see *An Historical Geography of England* ed. H. C. Darby (1948) chapters 9 and 10; P. Ramsey, *Tudor Economic Problems* (1963); W. K. Jordan, *Philanthropy in England 1480-1660* (1959); M. Campbell, *The English Yeoman under Elizabeth and the Early Stuarts* (1942); R. H. Tawney, *The Agrarian Problem in the Sixteenth Century* (1912) and *Religion and the Rise of Capitalism* (1926); L. B. Wright, *Middle Class Culture in Elizabethan England* (1935); C. Camden, *The Elizabethan Woman* (1952); J. Simon, *Education and Society in Tudor England* (1966); H. F. Kearney, *Scholars and Gentlemen, Universities and Society in Pre-industrial Britain* (1970); J. Thirsk (ed.) *The Agrarian History of England and Wales, 1500-1640* (1967); also *Essays in the Economic and Social History of Tudor and Stuart England* ed. F. J. Fisher (1961).

On religious issues see G. Baskerville, *English Monks and the Suppression of the Monasteries* (1937); M. C. Knowles, *The Religious Orders in England*, vol. III (1959); A. G. Dickens, *The English Reformation* (1964); H. Maynard Smith, *Pre-Reformation England* (1938) and *Henry VIII and the Reformation* (1048); E. G. Rupp, *Studies in the Making of the English Protestant Tradition* (1947); W. K. Jordan, *The Development of Religious Toleration in England* vol. 1 (1932); C. H. and K. George, *The Protestant Mind of the English Reformation 1570-1640* (1961); H. C. Porter, *Reformation and Reaction in Tudor Cambridge* (1958); A. O. Meyer, *England and the Catholic Church under Queen Elizabeth* (in German, 1911, trans. 1916); P. Hughes, *The Reformation in England* (3 vols. 1950, 1953, 1954); W. A. Clebsch, *England's Earliest Protestants* (1964); W. P. Haugaard, *Elizabeth and the English*

Reformation (1968); P. McGrath, *Papists and Protestants under Elizabeth I* (1967); P. Collinson, *The Elizabethan Puritan Movement* (1967); M. Walzer, *The Revolution of the Saints* (1966); B. R. White, *The English Separatist Tradition from the Marian Martyrs to the Pilgrim Fathers* (1971).

On naval and military affairs see J. S. Corbett, *Drake and the Tudor Navy* (2 vols. 1899); J. A. Williamson, *The Age of Drake* (1946); A. L. Rowse, *The Expansion of Elizabethan England* (1947); G. Mattingly, *The Defeat of the Spanish Armada* (1959); M. Lewis, *The Spanish Armada* (1960); C. G. Cruikshank, *Elizabeth's Army* (1946); L. Boynton, *The Elizabethan Militia* (1971); C. Falls, *Elizabeth's Irish Wars* (1950).

Among the numerous books on Tudor art and music perhaps the most interesting are : J. Lees-Milne, *Tudor Renaissance* (1951); E. Auerbach, *Tudor Artists* (1954); E. Mercer, *English Art 1553-1625* (1962); J. Buxton, *Elizabethan Taste* (1963); E. Waterhouse, *Painting in Britain 1530-1790* (1953); E. Croft-Murray, *Decorative Painting in England 1537-1837* vol. 1 (1962); D. Piper, *The English Face* (1957); C. Winter, *Elizabethan Miniatures* (1943); M. Whinney, *Sculpture in Britain 1530-1830* (1964); K. A. Esdaile, *English Church Monuments 1510-1840* (1946); S. Anglo, *Spectacle, Pageantry and Early Tudor Policy* (1969); R. Strong, *Holbein and Henry VIII* (1967) and *The English Icon, Elizabethan and Jacobean Portraiture* (1969); E. H. Fellowes, *English Madrigal Composers* (1921) and *The English Madrigal* (1925); J. Stevens, *Music and Poetry in the Early Tudor Court* (1961); also *The Autobiography of Thomas Whythorne* ed. J. M. Osborn (1961).

On various aspects of Tudor thought, among the more important books are : A. R. Hall, *The Scientific Revolution, 1500-1800* (1956); E. M. W. Tillyard, *The Elizabethan World Picture* (1953); Hardin Craig, *The Enchanted Glass: the Elizabethan Mind in Literature* (1935); C. S. Lewis,

English Literature in the Sixteenth Century (1954); H. Morris, *Elizabethan Literature* (1958); H. S. Bennett, *English Books and their Readers* (2 vols. 1952 and 1965); H. Haydn, *The Counter-Renaissance* (1950); J. B. Bamborough, *The Little World of Man* (1952); T. Spencer, *Shakespeare and the Nature of Man* (1942); J. F. Danby, *Shakespeare's Doctrine of Nature* (1949); M. M. Reese, *The Cease of Majesty* (1961); R. Kelso, *The Doctrine of the English Gentleman in the Sixteenth Century* (1929).

For political ideas see F. Le V. Baumer, *The Early Tudor Theory of Kingship* (1940); J. W. Allen, *The History of Political Thought in the Sixteenth Century* (1928); C. Morris, *Political Thought in England; Tyndale to Hooker* (1953); F. Raab, *The English Face of Machiavelli* (1963); W. H. Greenleaf, *Order, Empiricism and Politics; Two Traditions of English Political Thought 1500-1700* (1964); W. R. D. Jones, *The Tudor Commonwealth 1529-1559, A Study of the impact on the social and economic developments of mid-Tudor England upon contemporary concepts of the nature and duties of the commonwealth* (1970); J. K. McConica, *English Humanists and Reformation Politics under Henry VIII and Edward VI* (1965).

Outstanding among anthologies of Tudor writing are: C. H. Williams (ed.), *English Historical Documents, 1485-1558*; E. M. Nugent, *The Thought and Culture of the English Renaissance* (1956); A. Nicoll, *The Elizabethans* (1957); H. Haydn, *The Portable Elizabethan Reader* (1946); K. Muir, *Elizabethan and Jacobean Prose* (1956).

Conyers Read, *A Bibliography of British History, Tudor Period* (1933, revised 1959) is comprehensive and indispensable. But M. Levine *Tudor England 1485-1603* (1968), in the Cambridge Bibliographical Handbook, though smaller is more recent, very compact and most useful.

AUTHORITIES

CHAPTER I

1 J. M. Synge, Preface to *Poems and Translations* (1908)

2 Letter to T. L. Peacock, from Naples, January 26th, 1819.

3 *Wealth of Nations* (Everyman Edition), vol. ii, pp. 244-5.

4 Polybius, iv, 20-1, trans. E. S. Shuckburgh (London, 1889).

5 *Apologie for Poetrie* (Everyman Edition), p. 43.

6 *Boke of the Governour*, 1531 (Everyman Edition), p. 49.

7 ibid., p. 27.

8 ibid., p. 113.

9 ibid., pp. 82-3.

10 The Rev. William Dillingham in *The Commentaries of Sir Francis Vere* (Cambridge, 1657), p. 141.

11 See M. C. Bradbrook, *Shakespeare and Elizabethan Poetry* (London, 1951), p. 100.

12 See Hardin Craig, *The Enchanted Glass: the Elizabethan Mind in Literature* (Oxford, 1935), ch. v, *passim.*

13 *The Scholemaster*, ed. E. Arber (London, 1903), p. 64.

14 State Papers 12/192/22 cited in A. L. Rowse, *The England of Elizabeth* (London, 1951), p. 357.

15 R. H. Tawney and E. Power, *Tudor Economic Documents* (London, 1924), vol. i, pp. 20-1.

16 Heywood Townshend, *Historical Collections of the Four Last Parliaments of Queen Elizabeth* (London, 1680), p. 275.

17 See C. G. Cruikshank, *Elizabeth's Army* (Oxford, 1946), chs. i, vii and viii.

18 *Britannia*, trans. Philemon Holland (1637), p. 745.

19 J. M. Keynes, op. cit. (London, 1930), vol. ii, p. 154.

CHAPTER II

1 *Works of Sir Thomas Malory*, ed. E. Vinaver (Oxford, 1947), vol. i, pp. xiii-xx.

2 *An English Chronicle of the Reigns of Richard II, Henry IV, Henry V and Henry VI*, ed. J. S. Davies (Camden Soc., 1856), p. 97.

3 See C. L. Kingsford, *Prejudice and Promise in 15th Century England* (Oxford, 1923), pp. 58-64.

4 Dyer's Reports 188b, cited in F. W. Maitland, *English Law and the Renaissance* (Cambridge, 1901), p. 68.

⁵ The Case of the Earl of Oxford, 1625.
⁶ A. R. Myers, *England in the Late Middle Ages* (Pelican Books, 1951), p. 224.
⁷ St Francis of Assisi, " Canticle of the Sun ", in *The Little Flowers of St Francis* (Everyman Edition), p. 295.

CHAPTER III

¹ See E. A. Greenlaw, *Studies in Spenser's Historical Allegory* (Baltimore, 1932).
² S. Bentley, " Extracts from the Privy Purse expenses of Henry VII 1491-1505 ", in *Excerpta Historica* (London, 1831), pp. 85-133.
³ J. Leland, *Collectanea*, ed. T. Hearne (London, 1770), vol. IV, pp. 226-7.
⁴ Leland, op. cit., vol. V, p. 373.
⁵ *Memorials of Henry VII*, ed. J. Gairdner (Rolls Series, 1858), p. 223.
⁶ F. C. Dietz, *English Government Finance 1485-1558* (University of Illinois, 1920), pp. 80-2.
⁷ J. D. Mackie, *The Earlier Tudors* (Oxford, 1953), p. 218.
⁸ F. W. Brooks, *The Council of the North* (Historical Association, 1953), p. 4.
⁹ A. F. Pollard, Articles on " Council, Star Chamber and Privy Council under the Tudors ", in *E.H.R.*, vol. XXXVII, pp. 337-60 and 516-39.
¹⁰ *A Relation of the Island of England*, ed. C. A. Sneyd, (Camden Society, 1847), pp. 28 and 42-3.
¹¹ ibid., pp. 20-1.
¹² ibid., p. 24.
¹³ ibid., p. 32.
¹⁴ ibid., p. 46.

CHAPTER IV

¹ *Life and Death of Thomas Wolsey* (Temple Classics Edition), pp. 12-13.
² T. Stapleton, *Vita Thomae Mori*, cited in R. W. Chambers, *Thomas More* (London, 1935), p. 169.
³ W. Roper, Life of *Sir Thomas More* (Everyman Edition), p. 14.
⁴ P. S. Allen, *Opus Epistolarum Des. Erasmi Roterodami* (Oxford, 1906), vol. I, Ep. 215.
⁵ *Venetian Calendar*, II, 1287.
⁶ Quoted in E. G. Salter, *Tudor England through Venetian Eyes* (London, 1930), pp. 80-1.
⁷ *Venetian Calendar*, II, 920.
⁸ ibid., 918.
⁹ ibid., 624.
¹⁰ ibid., 138.
¹¹ ibid., 191.
¹² ibid., 288.
¹³ ibid., 739.
¹⁴ ibid., 330, 333, 400, 713, 1015.
¹⁵ See G. R. Elton, *The Tudor*

Revolution in Government (Cambridge, 1953), pp. 68-9.

16 Ibid.,

17 Calendar, State Papers, Milan, I, 395.

18 Quoted in B. White, Mary Tudor (London, 1935), p. 298.

19 Roper, Life of More, ed. E. V. Hitchcock (E.E.T.S., 1935), 67-8. Cf. Chambers, op. cit., pp. 193-4.

20 H. Maynard Smith, Pre-Reformation England (London, 1938), p. 162.

21 See R. W. Dixon, History of the Church of England (Oxford, 1895), vol. II, p. 56.

22 Letters and Papers of the Reign of Henry VIII, II, 2.

23 Venetian Calendar, III, 1028.

24 See Maynard Smith, op. cit., pp. 26-36.

25 Later Writings of Bishop Hooper, ed. C. Nevinson (Parker Society, 1852), p. 151. Cf. J. Gairdner in E.H.R., vol. XIX, 1904, pp. 98-9.

26 John Aylmer, An Harborowe for Faithfull and Trewe Subjects (Strasbourg, 1559) Sig. G. 3.

27 S. T. Bindoff, Tudor England (Pelican, 1950), p. 77.

28 Maynard Smith, op. cit., p. 48.

29 R. Keilway, Reports, ed. 1688, ff, 180-5; trans. A. Ogle in The Tragedy of the Lollard's Tower (Oxford, 1949), p. 153. Cf. L. & P., II, 1312, 1313.

30 Cavendish, op. cit., p. 122.

31 L. & P., IV, 3218. My translation from the French.

32 L. & P., IV, 4539.

33 L. & P., IV, 4597.

34 Venetian Calendar, IV, 365. Cf. Cranmer, Works (Parker Society, 1846), vol. II, p. 245, and Venetian Calendar, IV, 351, 418.

35 Venetian Calendar, II, 479.

36 Letters of Henry VIII, ed. M. St Clair Byrne (London, 1936), pp. 65-8.

37 See G. R. Elton, op. cit., passim.

38 Quoted in C. H. Firth, " The Ballad History of the Reigns of Henry VII and Henry VIII ", Transactions of the Royal Historical Society, 1907, p. 44.

39 Miscellaneous Writings and Letters of Thomas Cranmer, ed. J. E. Cox (Parker Society, 1846), pp. 326-7.

40 Hall's Chronicle, ed. C. Whibley (London, 1904) II, pp. 356-7.

41 Church History (Cambridge, 1655), bk. v, p. 254.

42 Hamilton Papers, ed. J. Bain (Edinburgh, 1892), vol. II, pp. 326-7.

43 L. & P., vol. XIX, pt. I, p. 214.

44 A. F. Pollard, Henry VIII (London, 1902), p. 375.

45 " The Practice of Prelates " in Tyndale's Expositions,

ed. H. Walter (Parker Society, 1849), p. 305.

CHAPTER V

1 J. G. Nichols, *Literary Remains of Edward VI* (Roxburghe Club, 1857), vol. i, pp. ccxiv-ccxvii.
2 Cited in *King Edward VI on the Supremacy*, ed. R. Potts (Cambridge, 1874), pp. xvi-xvii.
3 Nichols, op. cit., pp. xxxvi-xxxviii.
4 *The Letters of Stephen Gardiner*, ed. J. A. Muller (Cambridge, 1933), pp. 161-2.
5 Nichols, op. cit., pp. lxxiv.
6 " King Edward's Journal of his Own Reign ", in G. Burnet, *History of the Reformation in England* (1841 edition), vol. ii, pp. clxii and clxvi-clxvii.
7 Nichols, op. cit., p. cliii.
8 ibid., pp. clviii-clix.
9 Bishop Hooper to Henry Bullinger, March 27th, 1550. *Original Letters*, ed. H. H. Robinson (Parker Society, 1846), vol. i, p. 82.
10 Fuller, op. cit., p. 425.
11 Nichols, op. cit., pp. 75-6.
12 T. Heywood, *England's Elizabeth* (1631), p. 64; quoted in E. A. Greenlaw, *Studies in Spenser's Historical Allegory* (Baltimore, 1932), p. 102.
13 Fuller, op. cit., p. 424.
14 See Strype, *Ecclesiastical Memorials* (Oxford, 1822), ii, i, pp. 35-6.
15 Nichols, op. cit., p. cxxiii. Cf. S. Haynes, *Cecil State Papers* (London, 1740), p. 74.
16 Nichols, op. cit., p. cxv.
17 ibid., p. cxxxi.
18 Joye, *Defence of Marriage of Priests*, 1541, C, ii, a, quoted in J. F. Mozley, *Coverdale and His Bibles* (London, 1953), pp. 44-5.
19 *Spanish Calendar*, ix, p. 148.
20 See W. S. Hudson, *John Ponet* (Chicago, 1942), p. 49. Cf. L. Baldwin Smith, *Tudor Prelates and Politics* (Princeton, 1953), p. 253.
21 Mozley, op. cit., pp. 15-16.
22 Nichols, op. cit., p. 414.
23 ibid., p. 545.
24 ibid., p. 410.
25 J. Strype, *Ecclesiastical Memorials* (Oxford, 1822), vol. ii, pt. ii, pp. 429-37.
26 Quoted in A. F. Pollard, *England under Protector Somerset* (London, 1900), pp. 280-1.
27 Wriothesley, *A Chronicle of London* (Camden Society, 1875-7), vol. ii, p. 63.
28 Quoted in *Troubles connected with the Prayer Book of 1549*, ed. N. Pocock (Camden Society 1884), pp. xi-xii.
29 Nichols, op. cit., p. ccxxvii.
30 Fuller, *Church History*, bk. viii, sect. 1.
31 P. F. Tytler, *England under the reigns of Edward VI*

and Mary (London, 1839),
vol. I, p. 341.

32 Nichols, op. cit., pp. clxxvi.

33 Cited by S. T. Bindoff in " A
Kingdom at Stake 1553 ",
in *History Today*, September, 1953.

34 Fuller, op. cit., bk. VII, sect.
16.

CHAPTER VI

1 *Acts of the Privy Council*,
vol. III, pp. 348 *et seq.*

2 Foxe, *Acts and Monuments*,
(Ed. 1837) vol. VI, p. 354.

3 *Venetian Calendar*, IV, 60-1.

4 ibid., p. 288.

5 *Venetian Calendar*, V, 532.

6 ibid., cf. VI, pt. I, pp. 205-6.

7 H. Clifford, *Life of Jane
Dormer, Duchess of Feria*,
ed. J. Stevenson (London,
1887), p. 81.

8 ibid., pp. 167-9.

9 *The Proverbs, Epigrams and
Miscellanies of John Hey-
wood*, ed. J. S. Farmer
(London, 1906), pp. 300-1.

10 *Venetian Calendar*, V, 533.

11 *Venetian Calendar*, II, 1010.

12 T. Hearne, *Sylloge Epistolarum* (Oxford, 1716), p.
131.

13 *Ambassades de Messieurs de
Noailles en Angleterre*
(Leyden, 1763), vol. III,
pp. 280-2, cited in H. F.
M. Prescott, *Spanish Tu-
dor* (London, 1940), pp.
343-4.

14 Jane Dormer, op. cit., pp.
64-6.

15 F. Madden, *The Privy Purse
Expenses of the Princess
Mary* (London, 1831), pp.
cxliv, clxvii-clxix, appen-
dix IV, p. cxci.

16 J. P. Collier, *History of English Dramatic Poetry* (London, 1831), vol. I, pp.
265-6.

17 Madden, op. cit., p. 88.

18 N. H. Nicholas, *Privy Purse
Expenses of Henry VIII*
(London, 1827), pp. xxiii-
xxiv.

19 *Chronicle of Queen Jane and
Queen Mary*, ed., J. G.
Nichols (Camden Society,
1850), pp. 11-12.

20 G. Burnet, *History of the
Reformation* (London,
1841), vol. II, pp. 491-2.

21 Henry Machyn, *Diary*, ed.
J. G. Nichols (Camden
Society, 1848), p. 178.

22 Foxe, *Acts and Monuments*
(ed. 1684), vol. III, p. 25.

23 *Spanish Calendar*, XI, 228.

24 *Spanish Calendar*, XII, 230.

25 See L. Baldwin Smith, *Tudor
Prelates and Politics*
(Princeton, 1953), *passim*.

26 *The Lamentation of England*
1558, cited in Madden, op.
cit., p. cxlv, and John
Bradford's *Letter to Certain Lords of the Council*
in Strype, *Ecclesiastical
Memorials* (Oxford, 1822),
vol. III, pt. ii, p. 352.

27 *Spanish Calendar*, XI, 363-5.

28 Quoted from R. Tyler's tran-
scriptions of unpublished
Spanish documents in H.
F. M. Prescott, op. cit.,

pp. 353-4, and H. Simpson, *The Spanish Marriage* (London, 1933), p. 156.

29 *Venetian Calendar*, VI, 363.

30 Reminiscences of Cranmer's secretary, Ralph Morice, in *Narratives of the Days of the Reformation*, ed. J. G. Nichols (Camden Society, 1859), p. 259.

31 Autobiography of Thomas Mowntayne in *Narratives of the Reformation*, ed. J. G. Nichols (Camden Society, 1859).

32 *Venetian Calendar*, VI, 3, app. 136.

33 Foxe, op. cit., (ed. 1837-41), vol. VII, p. 86.

34 Prescott, op. cit., pp. 391-2.

35 Letter of Pedro Enriquez, quoted in M. A. S. Hume, "The Coming of Philip the Prudent", in *The Year after the Armada and other Historical Studies* (London, 1896), p. 169.

36 Foxe, op. cit., vol. VIII, p. 571. Cf. C. H. Garrett, *The Marian Exiles* (Cambridge, 1938), p. 11.

37 Garrett, op. cit., pp. 105-7.

38 Foxe, op. cit., (ed. 1684), vol. III, pp. 588-9.

39 See A. F. Pollard, *Political History of England 1547-1603* (London, 1910), p. 153. Cf. J. F. Mozley, *John Foxe and his Book* (London, 1940), pp. 223-35.

40 Foxe, op. cit., (ed. 1684), vol. III, p. 593.

41 *Narratives of the Days of the Reformation*, ed. J. G. Nichols (Camden Society, 1859), p. 70.

42 Foxe, op. cit., vol. III, p. 145.

43 ibid., vol. III, p. 147.

44 Prescott, op. cit., p. 417.

45 Foxe, op. cit., vol. III, p. 706.

46 *Venetian Calendar*, VI, pt. I, p. 299.

47 ibid., VI, pt. 2, pp. 1054-1058.

48 Jane Dormer, op. cit., pp. 69-70.

CHAPTER VII

1 Walpole, *Anecdotes of Painting*, chap. VII.

2 *History of England* (London, 1870), vol. V, pp. 3-4.

3 *Cal. Hatfield* mss., IV, p. 220.

4 John Aylmer, *An Harborowe for Faithfull and Trewe Subjects* (Strasbourg, 1559) sig. N1.

5 *Venetian Calendar*, VI, pt. II, p. 1059.

6 "Household Expenses of the Princess Elizabeth during her Residence at Hatfield 1551-1552", ed. Viscount Strangford in *Camden Miscellany II* (1853), pp. 30 and 47.

7 Quoted in F. Chamberlin, *The Sayings of Queen Elizabeth* (London, 1923), p. 300. Cf. J. Nichols, *Progresses of Queen Elizabeth* (London, 1823), vol. I, p. xiii.

8 Chamberlin, op. cit., p. 22.

Cf. Bacon " Apothegms ", in *Essays, Etc.* (London, 1902), p. 719.

9 As quoted in Sir J. E. Neale, *Elizabeth I and her Parliaments* (London, 1953), p. 149.

10 *Spanish Calendar: Elizabeth,* I, p. 181.

11 *Spanish Calendar*, 11, p. 364.

12 Sir James Melville, *Memoirs of his own Life* (Abbey Classics Edition), p. 52.

18 *Spanish Calendar*, I, p. 465.

14 ibid., 208.

15 ibid., 520-1.

16 Aubrey, *Brief Lives*, ed. Clark (Oxford, 1890) vol. 11, p. 139; *Notes of Conversations with Ben Jonson by William Drummond of Hawthornden*, ed. G. B. Harrison (London, 1923), p. 15.

17 See *Spanish Calendar*, I, 63 and 180; *Venetian Calendar*, VII, 330; a despatch from de Noailles in Haynes, *Cecil State Papers* (London, 1740), p. 215; and *Correspondence Diplomatique . . . de la Mothe Fénelon* (Paris and London, 1838), vol. 11, p. 122.

18 *A Tract on the Succession to the Crown* (1602), ed. C. R. Markham (Roxburghe Club, 1880), p. 40.

19 Melville, op. cit., p. 77.

20 *Venetian Calendar*, VII, 540; *Spanish Calendar*, 11, 491 and IV, 101-6 and 112.

21 Sir J. E. Neale, *Queen Elizabeth* (London, 1934), pp. 220, 239-40 and 244.

22 *Spanish Calendar*, I, 263.

28 ibid., p. 387.

24 " Fragmenta Regalia ", in *Somer's Tracts*, ed. W. Scott (London, 1809), vol. I, p. 253.

25 *Spanish Calendar*, III, 573, and IV, 87.

26 *Nugae Antiquae*, ed. H. Hetherington and T. Park (London, 1804), vol. I, p. 357.

27 *Foreign Calendar*, 1560-61, pp. 283, 319. Cf. *Spanish Calendar*, I, 175.

28 *Venetian Calendar*, VI, pt. II, 1058-9. Cf. ibid., V, 539, VII, 92 and IX, 565.

29 D'Ewes, *Journal*, p. 328.

80 W. Camden, *History* (London, 1675), p. 564. Cf. John Clapham, *Elizabeth of England*, ed. E. P. and C. Read (University of Pennsylvania, 1951), p. 89.

81 Harington, op. cit., vol. I, p. 357. Cf. ibid., pp. 11-14, 109 and 140-3.

82 Letter from Robert Cecil to Essex in T. Wright, *Queen Elizabeth and her Times* (London, 1838), vol. II, pp. 478-9. Cf. J. Nichols, *Progresses of Queen Elizabeth* (London, 1823), vol. I, p. ix.

88 Harington, op. cit., vol. I, pp. 115-18.

84 *Annals of the first four years of the reign of Queen Elizabeth*, ed J. Bruce (Camden Society, 1840), pp. 6-7.

85 Harington, op. cit., vol. I,

p. 358. Cf A. Strickland, *Life of Queen Elizabeth* (Everyman Edition), p. 544.

[86] *Venetian Calendar*, IX, 529.

[87] Harington, op. cit., vol. I, p. 359.

[88] Cited from P.R.O. *Paris Transcripts* by F. Chamberlin, op. cit., p. 305.

[89] *Correspondence Diplomatique de Bertrand de Salignac, de la Mothe Fénelon* (Paris and London, 1838), vol. I, p. 65. My translation.

[40] Harington, op. cit., vol. I, p. 345.

[41] Naunton, op. cit., p. 253.

[42] See Sir J. E. Neale, *The Elizabethan Political Scene* (British Academy Lecture, 1948), p. 11.

[43] *Works*, ed. J. Toland (London, 1747), p. 69.

[44] *Venetian Calendar*, VI, pt. II, pp. 1058-9.

[45] ibid., v, 539.

[46] Melville, op. cit., p. 55.

[47] Hayward, op. cit., p. 7.

[48] Naunton, op. cit., p. 252.

[49] John Clapham, op. cit., p. 88.

[50] Jacob Rathgeb, Secretary to the Duke of Wurtemburg, in *England as seen by Foreigners*, ed. W. B. Rye (London, 1865), p. 12.

[51] *Thomas Platter's Travels in England*, ed. C. Williams (London, 1937), p.192.

[52] Paul Hentzner, *A Journey into England*, trans. Horace Walpole (Strawberry Hill, 1757).

[53] André Hurault, Sieur de Maisse, *Journal*, trans. G. B. Harrison and R. A. Jones (London, 1931). Cf. *Venetian Calendar*, IX, 531-2.

[54] Venetian Calendar, VII, 628.

[55] ibid., IX, 565.

[56] See *Venetian Calendar*, IX, 238.

[57] Harington, op. cit., vol. I, p. 323.

[58] *Spanish Calendar*, III, 588.

[59] *Anecdotes and Traditions Illustrative of Early English History and Literature* ed. W. J. Thoms (Camden Society, 1839), p.47.

[60] *Spanish Calendar*, IV, 650.

[61] Melville, op. cit., p. 56.

[62] Naunton, op. cit., p. 269.

[63] *Calendar of Carew MSS. 1575-1588*, ed. J. S. Brewer and W. Bullen (London, 1868), p. 434.

[64] Clapham, op. cit., p. 41.

[65] *Spanish Calendar*, I, 127.

[66] ibid., 540.

[67] ibid., III, 188.

[68] *Cabala, sive Scrinia Sacra: Mysteries of State and Government, in Letters of Illustrious Persons* (London, 1691), pp. 343-4.

[69] Norfolk's Confession, quoted in Froude, *History*, vol. IX, p. 473.

[70] Fuller, *The Holy State* (London, 1840), pp. 255-6.

[71] J. Lyly, *Euphues' Glass for Europe*, 1580, ed. Bond, vol. II, p. 206.

[72] N. H. Nicholas, *Life of William Davison* (London, 1823), app. pp. 277-8.

[73] Froude, op. cit., vol. IX, p. 561.

[74] Harington, op. cit., vol. I, p. 356.

[75] ibid., pp. 318-19.

[76] ibid., pp. 362 and 355.

[77] *The Letters of Queen Elizabeth*, ed. G. B. Harrison (London, 1935), pp. 250-1.

[78] Quoted in M. Creighton, *Queen Elizabeth* (London, 1927), p. 103.

[79] D'Ewes, *Journals*, p. 46

[80] Strype, *Annals*, vol. II, pt. II, pp. 641-52, and *Sydney State Papers*, ed. A. Collins (London, 1746), vol. I, pp. 287-92.

[81] *Spanish Calendar*, I, 62.

[82] *Spanish Calendar*, I, 375.

[83] Fénelon, op. cit., vol. V, p. 232. My translation.

[84] Froude, *History*, vol. XI, p. 5 note.

[85] Harington, op. cit., pp. 171-2. Cf. *Spanish Calendar*, I, 405.

[86] R. Hakluyt, *Principal Navigations etc.* (Everyman Edition), V, p. 232.

[87] Quoted in Sir J. E. Neale, *The Elizabethan Age* (London, 1951), pp. 8-9.

[88] Birch, *Memoirs of the Reign of Queen Elizabeth* (London, 1754), vol. I, p. 483.

[89] D'Ewes *Journals*, p. 466.

[90] *Venetian Calendar*, IX, 223.

[91] T. Birch, op. cit., I, pp. 154-5

[92] Neale, *Queen Elizabeth*, p. 243.

[93] W. Camden, *History*, ed. 1675, p. 364.

[94] *Historical Collections of the four last Parliaments of Queen Elizabeth*, ed. Heywood Townshend (London, 1680), p. 263.

[95] D'Ewes, *Journals*, p. 466.

[96] F. Peck, *Desiderata Curiosa* (London, 1732), vol. I, pp. 64-6.

[97] Quoted in A. Cecil, *A Life of Robert Cecil* (London, 1915), p. 44.

[98] See *Memoirs of the Life of Robert Carey* (London, 1759), pp. 136-46; Birch, op. cit., vol. II, pp. 506-8; John Clapham, op. cit., pp. 96-102; Camden, op. cit., pp. 660-1; *Venetian Calendar*, IX, 558, 561, 564-5; A. Strickland, op. cit., pp. 694-703.

[99] "A.H." Introduction to Dudley Digges, *The Compleat Ambassador* (London, 1655), p. i.

[100] *Venetian Calendar*, VIII, p. 344.

[101] See A. M. Bell, "An Elizabethan Schoolboy and his Book", in *Gleanings after Time*, ed. G. L. Apperson (London, 1907), pp. 153-4.

GENEALOGICAL TABLE

Only the more prominent persons
in the Tudor story are shown

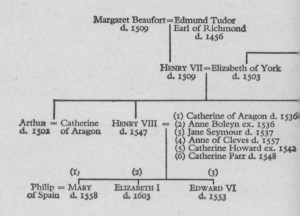

Margaret Beaufort = Edmund Tudor
d. 1509   Earl of Richmond
            d. 1456

HENRY VII = Elizabeth of York
d. 1509   d. 1503

Arthur = Catherine   HENRY VIII =   (1) Catherine of Aragon d. 1536
d. 1502   of Aragon   d. 1547   (2) Anne Boleyn ex. 1536
                                   (3) Jane Seymour d. 1537
                                   (4) Anne of Cleves d. 1557
                                   (5) Catherine Howard ex. 1542
                                   (6) Catherine Parr d. 1548

      (1)   (2)   (3)

Philip = MARY   ELIZABETH I   EDWARD VI
of Spain   d. 1558   d. 1603   d. 1553

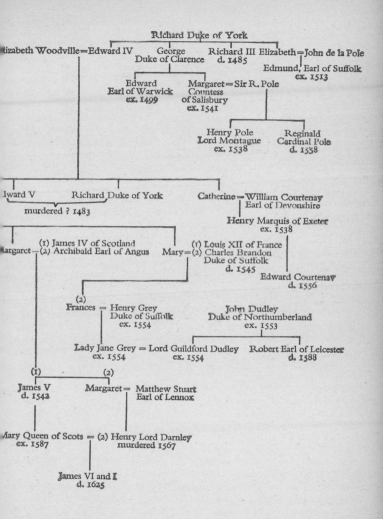

Richard Duke of York

Elizabeth Woodville=Edward IV   George   Richard III Elizabeth=John de la Pole
Duke of Clarence   d. 1485

Edmund, Earl of Suffolk
ex. 1513

Edward   Margaret=Sir R. Pole
Earl of Warwick   Countess
ex. 1499   of Salisbury
ex. 1541

Henry Pole   Reginald
Lord Montague   Cardinal Pole
ex. 1538   d. 1558

Edward V   Richard Duke of York   Catherine=William Courtenay
murdered ? 1483   Earl of Devonshire

Henry Marquis of Exeter
ex. 1538

Margaret—(1) James IV of Scotland Mary=(1) Louis XII of France
      (2) Archibald Earl of Angus   (2) Charles Brandon
                                Duke of Suffolk
                                d. 1545

Edward Courtenay
d. 1556

(2)
Frances = Henry Grey   John Dudley
      Duke of Suffolk Duke of Northumberland
      ex. 1554   ex. 1553

Lady Jane Grey = Lord Guildford Dudley Robert Earl of Leicester
ex. 1554   ex. 1554   d. 1588

(1)   (2)
James V   Margaret= Matthew Stuart
d. 1542   Earl of Lennox

Mary Queen of Scots = (2) Henry Lord Darnley
ex. 1587   murdered 1567

James VI and I
d. 1625

INDEX

Adams, William, 140
Aeschylus, 11, 39
Alençon, Duc d', 151, 157
Allerton, Ralph, 135
Ambassadors:
French, 99, 121, 144, 145, 148, 151
Imperial, 122, 124-5
Milanese, 72
Polish, 147
Scottish, 144
Spanish, 54, 104, 143, 144, 145, 153, 159
Venetian, 67-8, 70-2, 86, 117, 118, 120, 135-6, 149, 151
Anabaptists, 102, 132, 159
André, Bernard, 60
Angus, Earl of, 83
Aquinus, St Thomas, 49
Arcadia, 15
Architecture, 21-2, 44, 56, 73, 87
Aristotle, 48, 97
Armada, 18, 20, 30, 37, 38, 39, 124, 142, 154, 162, 167
Army, 24, 28, 102-3
Arthur, Prince, 57, 61
Ascham, Roger, 20, 121
Athens, 11-12, 87
Aubrey, John, 144

Bacon, Francis, 52, 58, 63, 65
Banister, John, 114
Barlow, William, 74
Beaufort, Lady Margaret, 66, 81
Bedingfield, Sir Henry, 156
Bible, 82, 90, 98, 99, 100, 135
Blount, Elizabeth, 81
Boacher, Joan, 102

Boleyn, Anne, 72, 79-83, 90, 93, 115, 117, 130, 137
Bond, Dr, 28
Bonner, Edmund, 102, 131, 135
Bosworth, 35, 66
Bothwell, Earl of, 144
Breton, Nicholas, 19
Bryan, Sir Francis, 119
Bucer, Martin, 110
Buckingham, Duke of, 82, 93
Burghley, *see* Cecil, William

Cadiz, 17, 142, 161
Calais, 96
Cambridge University, 29, 51, 160
Camden, William, 29
Canterbury, 74
Capel, Sir William, 64
Cardan, Jerome, 97, 98
Carew, Sir Peter, 153
Carey, Sir Robert, 167
Catherine of Aragon, 46, 62, 79, 81-3, 113, 117, 127
Cavendish, George, 70
Caxton, William, 41
Cecil, Robert, 138, 146, 148, 165-7
Cecil, William, 24, 27, 32, 33, 87, 105, 113, 140, 143, 144-6, 154
Cézanne, 21
Charles, Archduke, 153
Charles I, 27
Charles II, 27
Charles V, Emperor, 37, 84, 114, 115-16
Chaucer, Geoffrey, 50
Cheke, Sir John, 99, 127, 133

The British Monarchy

This series describes the evolution of the British monarchy from the Saxon and Norman kings to George V—their personalities and lives, their influence on their ages. Six volumes, each with twelve pages of photographs.

The Saxon and Norman Kings Christopher Brooke
'An illuminating and imaginative reconstruction of what it really meant to be a king in Saxon and Norman times. The essential merits of this book are its lightness of touch and its firm grounding in scholarship.' *The Economist*

The Plantagenets John Harvey
'A portrait gallery of medieval English sovereigns, illustrated with many splendid photographs. Learned, informative and entertaining.' *Daily Mail*

The Tudors Christopher Morris
'Brilliant . . . Mr. Morris's flair for the apt point or quotation is remarkable.' *History*

The Stuarts J. P. Kenyon
'A sardonic, witty, yet scholarly book, written with splendid gusto.' *Sunday Times*

The First Four Georges J. H. Plumb
'The vitality and frankness of a literary Hogarth. He is never dull or merely derivative.' *The Economist*

Hanover to Windsor Roger Fulford
'As accurate as it is amusing, and conspicuously fair in its judgments.' *The Times Literary Supplement*